THE POCKET IDIOT'S GUIDE™ TO

Beating Writer's Block

by Kathy Kleidermacher

ALPHA

A member of Penguin Group (USA) Inc.

ALPHA BOOKS

Published by the Penguin Group

Penguin Group (USA) Inc., 375 Hudson Street, New York, New York 10014, USA

Penguin Group (Canada), 90 Eglinton Avenue East, Suite 700, Toronto, Ontario M4P 2Y3, Canada (a division of Pearson Penguin Canada Inc.)

Penguin Books Ltd, 80 Strand, London WC2R 0RL, England

Penguin Ireland, 25 St Stephen's Green, Dublin 2, Ireland (a division of Penguin Books Ltd)

Penguin Group (Australia), 250 Camberwell Road, Camberwell, Victoria 3124, Australia (a division of Pearson Australia Group Pty Ltd)

Penguin Books India Pvt Ltd, 11 Community Centre, Panchsheel Park, New Delhi—110 017, India

Penguin Group (NZ), 67 Apollo Drive, Rosedale, North Shore, Auckland 1311, New Zealand (a division of Pearson New Zealand Ltd.)

Penguin Books (South Africa) (Pty) Ltd, 24 Sturdee Avenue, Rosebank, Johannesburg 2196, South Africa

Penguin Books Ltd, Registered Offices: 80 Strand, London WC2R 0RL, England

Copyright © 2007 by Penguin Group (USA) Inc.

THE POCKET IDIOT'S GUIDE TO and Design are trademarks of Penguin Group (USA) Inc.

International Standard Book Number: 978-1-59257-640-1
Library of Congress Catalog Card Number: 2006938603

09   08   07   8   7   6   5   4   3   2   1

Interpretation of the printing code: The rightmost number of the first series of numbers is the year of the book's printing; the rightmost number of the second series of numbers is the number of the book's printing. For example, a printing code of 07-1 shows that the first printing occurred in 2007.

Printed in the United States of America

Note: This publication contains the opinions and ideas of its author. It is intended to provide helpful and informative material on the subject matter covered. It is sold with the understanding that the author and publisher are not engaged in rendering professional services in the book. If the reader requires personal assistance or advice, a competent professional should be consulted.

The author and publisher specifically disclaim any responsibility for any liability, loss, or risk, personal or otherwise, which is incurred as a consequence, directly or indirectly, of the use and application of any of the contents of this book.

Most Alpha books are available at special quantity discounts for bulk purchases for sales promotions, premiums, fund-raising, or educational use. Special books, or book excerpts, can also be created to fit specific needs.

For details, write: Special Markets, Alpha Books, 375 Hudson Street, New York, NY 10014.

Contents

Introduction

It's been attributed to everyone from Dorothy Parker to Virginia Woolf to Robert Louis Stevenson, and it goes something like this:

> I don't enjoy writing. I enjoy having written.

Nevertheless, writing *can* be enjoyable. Hard sometimes, yes. Even frustrating. But is there anything quite like the feeling of getting swept up in the creative process, calling upon your whole self—your logical mind, your talent for language, your deepest emotions, your limitless imagination—and losing all track of time as you write? If you haven't had that feeling lately—if writing has started to seem like a chore or even fill you with dread—it's time to get back in the groove.

Writer's block can be rooted in, or related to, many things: lack of confidence, lack of motivation, lack of energy, procrastination, depression, anxiety. It can have mental, emotional, environmental, or physical aspects. But the good news is that even when the causes are complex, the solutions are often simpler than you think.

The emphasis in this book is on *solutions*. In addition to tips on everything from getting inspired to getting organized, these pages feature several sections packed with exercises and prompts that you can start using right away.

Extras

Throughout the book you'll find sidebars that emphasize and expand on the text—and sometimes provide a little entertainment:

> **Block Crock**
>
> These are examples of attitudes and beliefs that can stop a writer cold—followed by alternate ways of thinking that are more positive and constructive. You might recognize some of your own pitfalls here and learn how to avoid them in the future.

> **Breakthroughs**
>
> These quotes from authors and others should inspire you, make you think—and sometimes make you laugh.

> **Patience, Patience**
>
> The information in these boxes on writers who took a *long* time to finish their next book will remind you that art doesn't always come easily ... and will encourage you not to give up too soon.

Footnotes

Here you'll find random facts about the writer's block phenomenon. Check these boxes for points to ponder and some interesting trivia to share with your writer friends.

Acknowledgments

Thanks are due to Christy Wagner, Randy Ladenheim-Gil, Kayla Dugger, Jan Zoya, and Lisa Sklar for their great suggestions (and corrections), as well as to Kim Lionetti at BookEnds for making it happen.

Thanks also to my beloved husband—for his editorial assistance and for helping me through the big blocks.

Trademarks

All terms mentioned in this book that are known to be or are suspected of being trademarks or service marks have been appropriately capitalized. Alpha Books and Penguin Group (USA) Inc. cannot attest to the accuracy of this information. Use of a term in this book should not be regarded as affecting the validity of any trademark or service mark.

Chapter 1

Reboot!

In This Chapter

- What writer's block is ... and isn't
- Clearing your mind
- Getting into creative mode
- Easy unblocking exercises to start with

After a long, stressful day, I found myself traveling home on the train, feeling (once again) like my head was about to explode. My mind couldn't even form sentences—just fragments: *call back ... due Friday ... gotta fix that ... what day is ... come on, baby, do the locomotion ....* With too little sleep, too little food, and too much information to sort through, I started to crash, my vision going gray as I entered a brief state of almost sleeplike semiconsciousness. My head drooped for a moment; I lifted it back up after perhaps 5 or 10 seconds, and *voilà*—things were clear again. *Wow*, I thought. *My brain just rebooted.*

You might tend to think of your writer's block as a lack of ideas or a shortage of inspiration. It's actually a matter of too much, not too little. That is, there's too much stuff getting in the way, preventing you from getting a firm grasp on the ideas and the inspiration. After all, it's called writer's *block*, not writer's *blank*.

It's similar to a computer that's got too many programs running at once, overtaxing and slowing down the processor, causing all kinds of weird stuff to happen on your screen. When you're blocked—in writing or anything else—rebooting can be the key to getting past the problem and getting back to work, and you can learn to do it with just a little practice and guidance. It's better to do it on a regular basis than to let everything pile up until you crash.

This chapter focuses on ways to reboot your brain and beat the block, and concludes with some simple, basic writing exercises. Some of them might sound silly at first, but they can produce surprising results. And they're a gentle but effective way to work out the stiffness in those out-of-shape creative muscles.

Block Crock

I can't think of anything worth writing about.   Anything *is* worth writing about, if you're doing it with intelligence, honesty, passion, and your own unique point of view. The most mundane things—a sneeze, a job in a dessert shop, a jar of maraschino cherries—have inspired great poems by Dean Young, Daisy Fried, and Thomas Lux, respectively. We're all working with the same subject matter—human existence on planet Earth. What we do with it makes the difference.

Dump That Bad Data

If you want your brain to be open to creative ideas, excitement, positive motivation, and other good stuff, you need to make some room. Computer users are advised to periodically review their files and purge the outdated, useless, space-hogging material that's slowing down their machine. You can do the same thing with your brain to help you become more productive in your writing. Following are some suggestions to start ... or more appropriately, *restart*.

Banish *Some* Negative Thoughts

How do you know which of your negative thoughts you should listen to and which you should ignore? Well, a useful negative thought is usually ...

- Specific.
- Supported by real evidence.
- About something you can actually change.

If you're rereading a short story you wrote and keep muttering to yourself, *There's something cartoonish about this character,* chances are you're onto something, especially if you do another close read and notice that the character exhibits stereotypical traits, doesn't reveal much genuine emotion, and is wearing a Viking hat and a shaggy beard.

On the other hand, if your negative thoughts are running along the lines of *I have no talent* or *I'll never be published,* you can go ahead and trash them.

These sort of sweeping, unprovable generalities aren't doing you or anyone else any good.

Stop Writing

If you're having a hard time writing, it might be because you need to do something else right now. If you feel like you should be writing *all the time*, you're undermining yourself and setting yourself up for failure. Give yourself some time off. You'll be better off for it.

Take a Nap

Sometimes a nap is *the* thing you really need to clear your head—especially nowadays, when researchers estimate that about 20 percent of us are chronically sleep-deprived.

Plenty of information exists online about sleep deprivation's effect on the brain, but I can sum it up for you in three words: *it's not good*. And a well-functioning brain is very helpful when you're attempting a complex task like, say, writing.

Footnotes

The term *writer's block* was invented only about 50 years ago by a psychoanalyst who believed it was caused by deep-rooted anger over being weaned from the mother's breast. Well, that's one theory.

Put Up a Firewall

A lot of the bad data that's clogging up your head comes from the outside world. You need to filter all the noise and information that gets thrown at you on a daily basis, because an overwhelmed mind is not conducive to creativity. It's especially important to reject the sort of nonconstructive criticism and undermining comments sometimes aimed at writers, innocently or not.

Cut down on the claptrap surrounding you and seeping into your mind by taking some of the following steps.

Put the TV in Its Place

And I don't mean in the entertainment center! TV dominates our lives, sucking up hours and hours that could otherwise be devoted to writing. In addition, a lot of what's on TV isn't exactly intellectually or creatively nourishing.

Here are some ideas for breaking bad TV habits:

Watch only shows that serve your writing. That doesn't mean you have to TiVo every talk show that features a guest appearance by John Updike. Any programming that's well written and compelling gives you a deeper understanding of what makes things well written and compelling.

Seek out shows that relate in some way to the type of writing you want to do, whether it's mysteries, political opinion pieces, or novels about dysfunctional families.

If you find yourself watching something only because you don't feel like looking for the remote … look for the remote. And shut off the television.

Catch the news, but avoid the shout-fests.

Choose programs that make you laugh, cry, and think.

Skip the shows that only keep your attention by featuring a lot of shiny objects.

Commercials can take up about a quarter of your total viewing time. Hit the mute button and use some of those breaks to jot down a few notes or ideas inspired by what you just watched.

Don't head for the remote the moment you get home.

As for reruns, you're welcome to adopt my personal rule: comedy reruns are only allowed when I'm in dire need of a laugh. But drama reruns are simply not allowed, no matter how much I like Dr. House or good old Cagney and Lacey.

Minimize the Magazines

Magazines are seemingly everywhere—in waiting rooms, on the coffee table, in the bathroom …. But before you flip through one, ask yourself how much this particular publication is going to improve your life—including your writing life. Unless you're researching a novel based on the adventures of today's top supermodels, do you really need to keep up with everything they're doing? Will this women's magazine enrich your soul, or just make you feel fat?

Try replacing one glossy magazine a month with a different publication that features the best writing in your chosen genre. (Of course, if your dream is, in fact, to write about the entertainment industry, you should hold on to that *People* subscription.)

Patience, Patience

Ten years passed between Ernest Gaines's *A Gathering of Old Men* (1983) and *A Lesson Before Dying* (1993). The latter has more than a million copies in print, so that decade of work really paid off.

Take Things with a Grain of Salt

I once read that university-published journals never accept submissions from poets who don't have a Master of Fine Arts or an academic background. When I asked a panel of published poets about it during a Q&A session, they erupted in unison with "Nonsense!" (and some less-printable synonyms).

I was so afraid that my quest for publication was futile that I let this tossed-off comment on some website or another get to me ... temporarily, that is. If this statement had been in the submission guidelines of the actual journals, that would be one thing, but it wasn't. Which leads me to the next point ....

Consider the Source

When someone says something discouraging to you about your writing, there's a very good possibility that it's not really about your writing, but about that person's cynical or negative point of view. It's not that he particularly wants to discourage you; it's just that he has a deeply ingrained habit of looking at the downside.

The same goes for anything that qualifies as opinion rather than fact: for example, "Publishers only want young, sexy authors they can put on TV," especially if it's said by a cosmetic surgeon.

> **Block Crock**
>
> You have to be part of the in crowd to make it as a writer. If there's one field where being part of a clique doesn't count for too much, it's writing. In fact, being a bit of a hermit often adds to a writer's mysterious allure—look at J. D. Salinger! Don't be sucked in by the so-called glamour of the publishing world. It's about the writing, not the wine and cheese.

Admit That Writing Isn't a Super-Practical Career Choice

People are only too happy to voice their opinions when they find out you're a writer:

"That's a really hard field to break into."

"You can't make a living at that, can you?"

"I hope you have a backup plan."

These comments can have an insidious effect on your confidence if you allow them to. The best response is something along the lines of, "Yes, it can be tough going, but I really enjoy it. So I'm going to keep doing it—even if it doesn't make me rich."

Program Yourself to Write

Once you've cleared enough junk, you can start fresh and get into creative mode. (Keep in mind, though, that you can't do one big cleaning job and then never have to clean again. I've tried it with my bathroom, and believe me, it never works.)

Creativity, like a plant, flourishes only in certain conditions. You need to make a conscious effort to create those conditions if you want your talents to fight their way to the surface and find the light of day. The seeds of your wonderful work are already in there, and now that you've conditioned the soil, you just have to coax them to grow. Here are some ideas for doing just that.

Practice Zen

You needn't enter a monastery to enjoy the benefits of a meditative mind-set. Try this: while performing a mundane task, like washing dishes or sorting coins, focus mindfully on the job in front of you. If your brain starts chattering at you, let the thoughts float away, and return your attention to what you're doing.

Do this once and it might help you chill out and shift back into a creative groove. Do this on a regular basis, and it might change your life.

Block Crock

All the great artists are neurotic. Many artists may be quirky, different, or downright odd, or at least seem that way to nonartists. Thus, some people might label them "neurotic," but that doesn't have to mean self-destructive or emotionally unhealthy. If you're excusing self-destructive behavior by thinking *I'm just a typical neurotic writer*, cut it out. Embrace what makes you gloriously odd ... not what makes you miserable.

Try It Upside Down

Look at things from a different angle—literally. Lie on the floor and study the ceiling. At a party, stand in a corner and observe for a few minutes instead of mingling. Don't sit in "your" chair at dinner or your morning meeting. Lie on the grass at the park instead of sitting on a bench. Gaze through every window in your home, not just the usual ones.

There's a big world out there, with a lot of points of view that can inspire and inform your writing.

Sometimes you just need to take a step to the right or left to see them.

Footnotes

Harvard neurologist Alice Flaherty, in her book *The Midnight Disease*, speculates that writer's block might arise from a neurological problem—taking note that it shares some characteristics with Broca's aphasia, in which damage to the frontal lobe causes difficulty with producing language.

Be Brave

You know all that noise and blockage you've been getting rid of? It probably also served as a sort of mental suit of armor, keeping certain issues, thoughts, and emotions at bay. When you slow down, schedule some quiet time and open yourself to the big, complex world around you and your own pure, honest responses to it, it can be overwhelming at first.

This is where a lot of people get tripped up, retreating into the frustrating-but-familiar numbness. Don't get too freaked if you suddenly get a little teary-eyed at the sound of birds singing or if you get more irritated than usual at day-to-day annoyances. It's just the shock of change, and it will ease up. Plus, your new level of awareness will help you reach new heights in your writing.

Exercise: Get Warmed Up

After you've "reprogrammed" yourself, some simple writing exercises can help you start getting stuff down on paper. These exercises can take anywhere from 5 minutes to a half hour and are the equivalent of warm-up stretches. You can set aside a time each day to do one of them, or dip into them as you please. You might want to dedicate a small notebook to them and date each entry.

It's very important at this stage to write, not edit, so put the judging part of your mind aside for the time being. Don't go over the half-hour limit unless you find yourself on an unexpected creative path you really want to follow.

Here are some ideas to get you started:

Write a 250-word report titled "What I Did on My Summer Vacation."

Open a dictionary, close your eyes, and randomly pick out three words. Now write something with those three words in it.

They say it's impossible to describe a sunset. Describe a sunset.

Try to write a really, really bad poem.

Write about someone you wanted to be like as a teenager. Don't include yourself at all; just describe him or her, as if you were introducing a character in a novel.

Write, quickly, a paragraph that describes an activity you did today, using *I*. Turn the page over. Now write about the same activity again, using *you*. Then once more, using *he* or *she*. When you're finished, reread them all and note whether any additional differences exist among the three versions.

Write a dialogue between two people on the topic of a hat.

Patience, Patience

Jeffrey Eugenides took 9 years to complete *Middlesex* after publishing *The Virgin Suicides* in 1993.

Write exactly what's on your mind right now for 10 minutes without stopping to think.

Write about a person you know and try to convey what he or she is like in five sentences—without using any adjectives.

Describe your apartment or house in a way that makes it sound unpleasant and uncomfortable. Then describe it in a way that makes it sound pleasant and comfortable. Both descriptions should be completely factual.

Imagine yourself landing on a planet in another galaxy in some far-off age of space travel. Describe what it looks like when you step out of the starship.

Write an eight-line poem about a single color.

Write an internal monologue by a character caught in a traffic jam.

You probably have a story about some amusing or dramatic incident in your life that you've told to numerous people but have never written down. Write it down.

If you grew up in a city, write about what you, as a child, thought it must have been like to grow up in the country and why you thought so. If you grew up in a suburban or rural area, write about your childhood impression of city life.

Write a short story, no more than three pages long, that starts out with someone finding an itemized store receipt in the street.

Write about an experience you had in which bad weather played an important role.

Pretend you have to give a 1-minute speech about an issue you care about and write it. (The good part is, you don't actually have to give the speech!)

Sit at a sidewalk café, or anyplace where plenty of people walk by, and write what comes to your mind as you watch them pass.

Once you've stretched your mind on these exercises, you might feel a little more ready to ease back into your own projects. You might also have learned that sometimes the simplest (or silliest) things can inspire very interesting work.

The Least You Need to Know

- It's a *block*, not a *blank*. The ideas are there; they're just blocked from view.

- Trash bad stuff in your mind to make room for good stuff—the creative stuff, the inspirational stuff.

- Anxiety is natural—and temporary. If you're experiencing it, you can work through it.

- Building courage, looking at the world from new angles, and calming your mind can all help program you to become a better writer.

Environmental Block

In This Chapter

- Finding the place to write that works for you
- Gathering the supplies to make the job easier
- Solving organizational problems that slow you down

Few pursuits give you as much flexibility and freedom as writing in terms of where, when, and how you can do it. Throw a pen and a small notebook into your pocket, and you can write anywhere—on a plane, a park bench, a mountaintop. Great books have even been written in prison. Nowadays, carrying a notebook computer around with you isn't much more difficult than carrying an actual notebook—although it is a bit more expensive. And computers are available for public use in libraries, universities, and Internet cafés. If the electricity goes out, you can write by flashlight or candlelight. (Just don't let the paper get too close to the candle.)

This flexibility and freedom writing provides can be a blessing, but it can also be a curse. If you have a tendency to put off writing, the fact that you can always do it at another time or place makes it easier to rationalize procrastination. (Why grab this particular opportunity to write when there are plenty more right around the corner?) And the very fact that there are so many options to choose from can make it hard to identify which options work best for you personally. Your surroundings, the equipment you use, and your habits might be greatly affecting your productivity, and you might not even realize it.

However, there are ways to experiment, and guidelines to follow, that can help you identify your ideal writing environment, maximize your output, and ultimately, improve the quality of your work. This chapter tells you about them—and might lead you to some simple changes that make a big difference.

Your Writing Space(s)

The most famous writing space in the world is almost certainly Henry David Thoreau's Walden Pond. In 1845, he built himself a wooden cabin on an unspoiled plot of land in Massachusetts. (One thing that certainly helped Walden Pond become a lasting symbol of the writer's ideal workspace is the fact that Thoreau titled one of his books *Walden, or Life in the Woods*.) The challenge in modern times is to find our own Walden Ponds—places where we can hear ourselves think, find inspiration, draw energy from the space around us, and focus on our creative task.

Patience, Patience

William Gaddis's first novel, *The Recognitions*, was published in 1952. His second, *JR*, arrived in 1971. (*JR* was more than 700 pages long, though, so that could account for some of the delay.)

Scores of places and programs are devoted to offering writers just that. Some are quite renowned, like the 100-year-old MacDowell Colony, which hosts artists of all kinds and is able to admit only one in six applicants. But for beginner-level writers who can afford the expenditure of time and money, plenty of organizations provide more accessible opportunities to attend what may be called retreats, workshops, seminars, conferences, or colonies. Many colleges and universities, particularly those with well-known graduate writing programs, run special summer gatherings, many of which feature small workshops with prominent authors, lasting a weekend, a week, or more.

Some retreats take place in exotic or lush locales, combining the appeal of writing and learning with elements of travel and vacation. Others offer bare-bones accommodations, promising no luxuries except the most important one: time to write. You can find out what's out there by visiting writersdigest.com/conferences or by checking listings in the annual volumes *Writer's Market*, *Poet's Market*, or *Short Story Writer's Market*. *Poets and Writers Magazine* also lists conferences in the back of each issue, with a special section on them every year in its March/April issue.

> **Patience, Patience**
>
> It took Tom Wolfe 11 years to put out his next novel, *A Man in Full*, after 1987's *The Bonfire of the Vanities*.

A well-chosen writing getaway can be a terrific boost and a learning experience for the serious writer who needs to get back on track after an extended block. But because they can be costly and provide only a temporary haven, it's extremely important to find—or create—a physical space that can serve as your own Walden Pond on a daily basis. Companies spend millions of dollars to design workspaces and procedures that help their employees produce more and better work, because they've learned what an important role the environment plays in a person's daily activities. You, too, can design your workspace to help you beat your block and increase your output.

In the following sections, I give you some questions to ask, experiments to try, and suggestions for solutions that you might not ever have thought of in your quest for finding your perfect writing space.

Are You a Creature of Habit?

We're all creatures of habit to some extent, and although the term is sometimes used in a derogatory way, it's not necessarily a bad thing. But if you experience chronic writer's block, you might be indulging in either too much or too little habitual behavior.

Examine the jobs you've held. Did you tend to perform better in structured environments, on a regular schedule, or did you really shine when things were a little unpredictable and you had to think on your feet? Do you prefer hanging out with a few close friends, or going to a big party? If you're stranded somewhere by bad weather or other circumstances, do you tend to consider it stressful or fun?

Block Crock

I can only write at my desk, in the evening, with a cup of coffee.   If your writing routine works for you, great. But if you're getting blocked, a change of scenery might do you good. Don't presume that you simply "can't" write in the early morning or at the library. Shake it up a little!

If you said "yes" to the first choice in each question, you might do better writing in the same place, at the same time, every day. If you identified more with the second choices, you might require a little more stimulation and find it useful to look for new writing spaces to keep your juices flowing. And if you answered both ways—sometimes the first choice, sometimes the second—you can try mixing structure with spontaneity: write at your kitchen table each evening, but also treat yourself to a little writing adventure once or twice a week.

Are You Easily Distracted?

If you're like me, your answer to this question probably won't be "yes" or "no," but "sometimes." There are days when I can sit in a bustling diner with clattering plates, shouts from the kitchen, and piped-in music and still be so caught up in my writing that my coffee goes cold beside me. (Thank heavens for free refills.) At other times, I can have my attention drawn away by the slightest breeze.

The key is to be aware and responsive to your own level of distractibility at any given time. If, say, you're trying to write at Starbucks and find yourself repeatedly examining the pastry case instead of completing paragraphs, you might be too easily sidetracked right now to get any work done in this kind of atmosphere. Either that or you're hungry and should get yourself an espresso brownie.

But if the brownie doesn't help, don't give up and say, "I just can't write today." Move to a quieter spot, perhaps a library or park nearby, and see if the situation improves.

The Air You Breathe

You're likely to have clearer ideas and write clearer sentences if you're breathing clear air. Open a window or door. If you suffer from allergies or sinus problems, ask your doctor about medications or devices that can help.

If you're a smoker and habitually light up when working, you might wind up with nagging headaches, especially if your workspace isn't well ventilated.

Try not to bring your ashtray and cigarettes into your writing room with you. You might find that if they're not there, you'll get caught up enough in your story or poem that you won't even miss them. Or move to a place where you can't smoke, like a coffee shop. You can always take a smoke break after you finish that chapter.

> **Block Crock**
>
> **I can't write without smoking!**
> I thought so, too. I was wrong. I write on the job, and when my company moved from a smoking to a nonsmoking building, I thought I was a goner. Instead, I got used to it within days, and the same thing happened when smoking was banned in the cafés where I did my personal writing. If a walking chimney like me can do it, so can you.

See the Light!

Straining or squinting is not going to help your concentration level, so be sure you're working with comfortable lighting. Minimize the glare coming off your computer screen by positioning it away from direct sun or artificial light. Dusting off the monitor periodically also helps reduce glare.

Sound Off ... or On

Unexpected noises can rattle our nerves more than expected ones do. That's why someone on a cell phone in the background can be so much more aggravating than two people conversing in the background. An in-person conversation blends into an ongoing, continual noise that you can tune out, while a person on a cell phone startles you again and again with talking punctuated by silences of unpredictable length.

Clearly, trying to write with someone on a cell phone nearby is probably not a good idea. But what about other background sounds? It can be tricky.

Music, for example, can help you focus, or make it impossible to focus. You'll need to experiment for yourself to see what works for you. I find that the more dynamic and dramatic—in other words, the more unpredictable—the music, the more it distracts me. Conversely, familiar songs with a steady beat, and few variations in volume and pitch, can soothe my soul and grease the creative wheels. (I like to haul out the old disco compilations.) If you work in public places a lot, do some research on headphones, including the noise-canceling or sound-isolating kind. They can be pricey, but pay for themselves in increased productivity.

The important thing is to minimize sudden sounds that can throw you off-kilter. Soundproofing and white-noise machines can be pretty expensive, but you might be able to achieve similar effects with an air conditioner or fan.

And to avoid other noisy distractions, unplug your phone or turn down the ringer, or try writing in the early morning or late evening when the world around you isn't humming quite so loud.

If you're really stuck, visit a music store and treat yourself to a pair of earplugs. Many offer plugs cheap or even free, to protect tender young ears from the ravages of high-decibel live shows.

Breakthroughs

Appealing workplaces are to be avoided.

—Annie Dillard, arguing in *The Writing Life* that without interesting things to look at, your imagination will be forced to get to work faster

What Resources Do You Have Nearby?

Scan your town or neighborhood. Keep an eye out for parks, beaches, playgrounds, picnic areas, libraries, community centers ... any place that could potentially offer some isolation and refuge, especially during less-busy off-hours.

Closer to home, if you live in an apartment building, find out whether you can get (safe) access to the roof.

Relocate

Moving might not be an immediate option, depending on your current employment or financial situation, but if you're living somewhere you don't like, it can affect your writing, particularly if there's too much noise or if your place doesn't offer an area that's conducive to getting work done.

If you can't make a change right now, keep this question in the back of your mind for future moves: *Will this be a good space for me as a writer?*

Your Equipment

Someone once told me that I wrote differently in longhand than I did on a computer. It makes sense, I guess. I'm sure I'm a bit more free-form and adventurous when I know I can revise and delete to my heart's content with just the touch of a few buttons. And because my (literal, not figurative) writing muscles seem to have atrophied severely since the dawn of the electronic age, I'm especially motivated to be deliberate and concise when I'm holding a pen nowadays. Otherwise, my right arm is going to start aching pretty quickly. And even without any aches, writing by hand tends to go slower, which can be frustrating when the ideas are really pouring forth.

But beyond the pen-versus-keyboard question, your writing gear is an important part of your work environment. As I noted earlier, you don't need much equipment to write, but a few well-chosen items can certainly make the job easier.

In this section, I offer a list of things that might help you get started—and, just as important, keep at it. See if any of the following might be worthwhile additions to your writing space.

Reference Books

The Internet is an astounding research tool that has, understandably, replaced printed books in many cases. Aside from the obvious advantages, online sources are especially preferable when it's important that your information be as up-to-date as possible.

But there are still some advantages to printed references. Established books, from established publishers, are reliably authoritative; you don't have to search through a lot of questionable search results to find a source you can trust. Plus, books don't have pop-ups. And when you pick up a serious reference book, you don't risk following a series of links so that you somehow wind up reading a dopey, time-wasting book instead. Books are also handy when you're working in your word processing program and don't necessarily want to keep switching from one window to another—sometimes it's easier just to keep a book or three open at your side.

Footnotes

The very existence of writer's block is a topic of debate among writers. Some insist that the term is just an excuse for avoiding writing. (Then again, the fact that someone is avoiding writing could be construed as a type of writer's block ... and "just do it" isn't always the most helpful advice.)

Don't discount the value of the old-fashioned "real book" when it comes to writing. If you're working on something for a publisher, you might need to follow a specific stylebook, but for general writing, you'll want to keep frequently used references nearby. In addition to a dictionary, a thesaurus, and a grammar guide, you can find amazing specialty references that seem custom-made for your field of interest. To find some, plug a few appropriate combinations of keywords (*Regency England, cowboys, medical, medieval history,* and the like, plus *terms, encyclopedia, guide,* or *dictionary*) into your favorite online bookselling site or search engine and see what turns up.

Notebooks, Notebooks Everywhere

A common piece of advice given to writers is to keep a notebook nearby. I take that a step further: keep *many* notebooks nearby. Stash them like a squirrel stashes nuts:

- One in each room of your home, within arm's reach of the place you usually sit
- One in each knapsack, pocketbook, laptop case, or whatever other bag you schlep around
- One at your workplace, in your locker, in the car …

You get the idea. And of course, there should be a pen right next to each one.

I can't count the promising ideas or bits of just-right wording I've lost because I told myself, *I'll get up in a minute and find my notebook.* I've learned, and I'm passing the lesson on to you.

> **Patience, Patience**
>
> **If it's good, I'll remember it.** Don't count on it. You're a busy person, and memory can be very unreliable. Write it down. Now.

When it's all but impossible to keep a notebook nearby—during your morning run, for example— carry a cell phone at least. Then you can recite your idea or perfect sentence into your voicemail to be transcribed later.

A Cabinet for Your Files

You're far more likely to follow up on an idea or writing project you came up with 6 months ago if your notes and scribblings from back then are at your fingertips than if you have to search through scattered piles to find them.

Get organized!—and get a metal two- or three-drawer file cabinet from your local office-supply store. They're fairly inexpensive, and some are made of cardboard, in case you're on an especially tight budget. You can even get a small file case with a handle on it—easy to grab and carry in case of emergency.

Backups—Digital and Otherwise

If you're fighting writer's block, you don't need little annoyances that give you an easy excuse to stop working. Keep backup supplies of printer paper, pens, ink cartridges, disks, and whatever else you don't want to run out of right in the middle of the stunning climactic scene of your novel. Keep some pencils in your drawer … and a pencil sharpener.

And speaking of backup, don't forget to keep extra copies of your work. There's not much more discouraging than suddenly losing the first 20 or 50 or 200 pages of your book. You can prevent disaster by …

- Printing out your work.
- Making a photocopy to be kept at another location.
- E-mailing the document to another computer (perhaps one belonging to a trusted family member or writer friend).
- Using an external hard drive.
- Saving your work on a CD-ROM or floppy disk.

Don't be complacent. Recovering data after a computer crash can be very expensive or downright impossible. And it's not just crashes that can make your pages disappear. A New Orleans writer I met told me that the only reason her work still existed was because her computer happened to be on the second floor of her house when Hurricane Katrina hit.

Organization

Any job—including writing—is easier when it's done in an organized fashion. You waste less time, and experience less frustration, when you have a plan—increasing your frustration level when you're struggling with writer's block is the last thing you want to do!

You might feel that a neat desk is a sign of a dull, stuffy bureaucrat instead of a writer, but do yourself a favor and save the drama and excitement for the page. If you want to be in control of your writing, the first step is to be in control of your process and your environment.

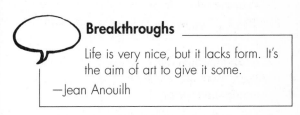

Breakthroughs

Life is very nice, but it lacks form. It's the aim of art to give it some.

—Jean Anouilh

Even if you like things a little messy, you should try to maintain some kind of system so there's a method to your madness. With that in mind, in the following sections, I share some tips to make your work go more smoothly—resulting in increased productivity and better results for you.

A Place for Everything

If you've got a designated writing space, set it up so everything you need is right there and easy to find.

If all your printer paper, staples, paper clips, or pens are in one place, you'll not only be able to grab them in seconds, but you'll also know when you're running low and need to buy a new supply. All kinds of trays and desktop files can help you sort things out.

For example, you might keep an upright file on your desk, with slots allotted to the following:

- Copies of submissions you've sent out
- Unfinished pieces you want to continue working on
- Articles you've clipped that might inspire future projects
- Articles you've clipped for reference on a current project
- Blank paper for quick printer-tray refills

If you don't want it all on your desktop, you can neatly file it away in your file cabinet. (You did get one of those, didn't you?)

A Digital Place for Everything

Take advantage of your computer's capabilities to help you get organized. I'm not even talking fancy software here. Something as simple as clearly labeled folders and subfolders can keep your writing work easily accessible and logically organized when you want to find something quickly. (If you don't know how to create files or folders, find out from a friend or instruction manual. It's not hard at all.)

When saving your documents, name them so different drafts remain together in alphabetized file lists:

Shaggy Dog Story 01, Shaggy Dog Story 02, etc. This not only helps you find them faster, it also makes for quicker and easier backups.

Know When to Folder 'Em

Whether they're digital or the old-fashioned kind, keeping separate folders for multiple, simultaneous writing projects is a good idea. Small obstacles can create big problems for someone battling writer's block, and you don't want to lose your enthusiasm while shuffling through a mess of materials. When all your notes, references, and drafts for Project A are together in the Project A folder, Project A will seem a lot less intimidating.

Your Own Personal Database

Whether you do it on a spreadsheet or in a note-book, you'll want to keep track of what you're sending out to whom. Create a chart on which you can note titles, dates of submission, places of submission, and responses received. You'll also want a column for expenses like contest entry fees and postage if they constitute deductible business expenses for you.

Patience, Patience

Jayne Anne Phillips published the story collection *Fast Lanes* in 1984—and followed up with the novel *Shelter* 10 years later.

What's great about keeping such records is that not only do they enable you to stay on top of the submission process, but they also let you look at all you've accomplished. Because even if you haven't gotten that first acceptance yet, just finishing things and sending them out is something to cheer about.

Your Own Personal Post Office

If you send out a fair amount of submissions, the United States Postal Service has ways to make your life easier. Postal scales are available for about $40, and you can use your computer to do everything from finding ZIP codes to calculating the necessary postage, paying for it, and printing it out.

Don't wind up missing deadlines or letting timely ideas go stale just because you're too busy. Visit www.usps.com or stop into your local P.O. and find out what great new services can help you with your writing career. You can also do a little comparison shopping and check out such private shippers as FedEx, UPS, and DHL.

Special Bulletin!

If your work setup allows it, keeping a bulletin board in front of or next to your writing desk can be a huge help. If not, you can do what I do—tape things to the wall. I've got the outline of this book hanging up right next to me, and it really comes in handy.

In addition to quick references and information, like a list of words you tend to misspell or the family tree of the characters in your story, you can put anything you want up there that will serve to inspire you: a poem you love, an encouraging quote, a picture of the mansion you're going to buy when your novel hits the best-seller list ....

Synopsis, Outline, Summary, Table of Contents ...

Everyone has individual preferences when it comes to "working from an outline." And of course, not every piece of writing requires one. But if you've rejected the idea in the past, give it some reconsideration.

Block Crock

Outlines are boring and pointless. Don't disrespect your own work. A novel, a short story, or even a brief essay is a complex creation. Give it the care and forethought it deserves.

As with neat desks and regular schedules, some people seem to think it's just not writerlike to prepare an outline. Maybe it brings back bad memories of doing high-school book reports. (Remember "topic sentences"? Ugh.) But what's important is what works, and sketching out your piece before you plunge into it can eliminate a lot of writer's block. It gives you something to hold on to so you don't lose your way, and it helps you keep your overall goals clear in your head. It can prevent you from writing something in a frenzy of inspiration and later thinking *Why didn't I include such and such?* Outlining also helps you figure out the most effective order to put your ideas and paragraphs in.

When you're stuck, a table of contents can be a way of "writing without writing"—that is, sorting out the structure of your project and making real progress on it, without the immediate pressure of crafting publishable sentences. And if you're afraid it will make you feel too restricted, just keep in mind that there's no law against changing your outline as you go along!

The Least You Need to Know

- Your work environment and habits make a big difference in your level of productivity.
- Experiment to find out which settings and atmospheres get your creativity flowing.
- Disorganization makes it harder to accomplish your goals—including your writing goals. Get organized and you might break through what's blocking you.

Chapter 3

Daily Skill Builders

In This Chapter

- The importance of practice
- Mastering the mechanics of writing
- Taking in the world—and turning it into art

You probably encounter a lot of advice in a day—
not just about writing but about any type of
endeavor—that encourages you to think positively,
believe in yourself, and reach for the stars. I'm all
for those things, but sometimes the enthusiastic pep
talks gloss over the fact that success takes more than
just self-esteem. It takes practice.

Someone who's coasting on confidence alone eventually has the wind knocked out of him. For example, I was always labeled a "smart kid" in school,
so I wasn't worried when I got my first office job.
Imagine how embarrassed I was when I actually had
to be taught how to use a paper clip.

Unfortunately, creative writers can be particularly
susceptible this problem, especially if they've
avoided taking any classes or showing their work to
objective observers, or if they only write once in a

while "when inspiration strikes." Having an overly mystical, "you're born with talent or you're not" viewpoint about writing only makes it worse. (It also makes you prone to wasting a lot of your time on those silly, hand-wringing, *Maybe I just wasn't born to do this* pity parties.)

One musician I know resisted taking lessons for many years, feeling that it "wasn't rock and roll." Lessons were for stuffy classical types, not kick-butt guitarists who improvised wild solos in front of screaming crowds. The thing was, after he gave in and actually took some lessons, he rapidly improved his skills and wound up recording a CD (and actually selling a few copies). Some people might indeed be born with raw talent, but raw talent alone gets them nowhere if they're unwilling to learn and practice.

Block Crock

You're either born a writer or you're not. Oh, yeah? Do you know a kid who learned his alphabet without any help? You learned your alphabet with help, and you learn what you can do with that alphabet with others' help throughout your life—even if it's only from the authors who came before you and left you their books to read as examples.

This chapter focuses on things you can do every day to build your skill and goes hand in hand with

Chapter 4, which focuses on ways to build your confidence. But always bear in mind that the best way to build your confidence is to build your skill.

Exercise: Master Your Craft

There's always room to improve. The exercises in this section focus on the mechanical skills writers employ: the ability to choose the right words, to structure and pace their story, to clarify their meaning, and more.

Good writing involves a lot of different aspects, from basics like grammar and vocabulary to complex challenges like plotting, pacing, characterization, and dialogue. Chances are you have strength in some of them and weakness in others. Approach these exercises like a balanced, full-body workout, so you don't wind up with powerful plots and spindly little characters (or the other way around).

Take a Sentence Apart

And then put it back together again. Soldiers do it with rifles, mechanics do it with engines, and you should do it with your essential tool. In the flow of creative excitement, we often write as quickly as possible. Then, when the excitement is over, we're afraid to go back and look too closely at what we've written. (What if it turns out not to be as great as we think?) Or we might get bored and want to move on to something new.

Footnotes

The poet Samuel Coleridge had one of the earliest recorded cases of writer's block, which he described as "an indefinite, indescribable Terror."

Take out something you've written recently, and put one of your sentences under a microscope. Is that the best noun, verb, or adjective you could use? Does the sentence sound smooth and musical, or dissonant and clunky? Is this clause in the best place it could be? Could someone read this and interpret it the wrong way?

If you make a habit of doing this now, you'll come to understand the subtleties of language on a whole new level—and you'll be a lot less likely to need extensive editing in the future.

Read at a Distance

I've sat in workshops as people read a poem I wrote—a poem I thought was perfectly clear—and speculated on what it meant, coming up with interpretations I didn't remotely intend. Of course, my first thought was, *How could these people not get this?* But as the discussion continued, it became quite obvious how they could not get it. It *wasn't* perfectly clear after all.

When we write, we tend to read our work from our own point of view. Not just point of view in the sense of our beliefs and opinions, but, quite literally, our point of view. We see it from exactly where we're standing, and it all seems obvious to us.

Breakthroughs

Bad authors are those who write with reference to an inner context which the reader cannot know.

—Albert Camus

If we're using our own lives for material, we know things about the background of the story (or the poem, or the essay) that enable us to fill in the gaps. If it's fiction, we probably built a vivid picture of the characters and action in our head as we were writing it. We know which "she" we're referring to—but a reader who has just been introduced to three different female characters might not. When we write "the gray dome overhead," we're picturing the sky we're describing, but someone coming upon this phrase could easily picture a dome-shaped ceiling painted gray and presume that the piece takes place indoors, not outside. Sometimes we throw in a bit of irrelevant information just because we remember it as "part of the picture," but its inclusion leads readers to presume it's something meaningful and give it more weight than it deserves.

Take a piece you've written and read it as if you were a stranger seeing it for the first time. And if you find it hard to do so, ask someone else to read it and tell you exactly what it means. You might be surprised.

Play *Taboo*

The board game *Taboo* challenges players to make their teammates guess a word without using the most obvious words to describe it. For example, you might have to get them to guess "sky"—but without using words like *up, blue, clouds, sun,* or *moon.*

Play your own game of "writing *Taboo.*" Write about your fond feelings for someone without using the words *nice, friend, like, love,* or *connection.* Write about a winter scene without using the words *snow, ice, frozen, white,* or *still.*

Write a Joke

Comedians know humor is a tricky art. One wrong—or wrongly placed—word or one missing piece of information, and the joke meets with painful silence.

Write a joke you recall hearing or a brief, humorous anecdote about something that happened to you or someone else. Tinker with it until it reads the funniest. Asking different friends to read different versions along the way, and seeing which provoke smiles or laughs, can make it easier to identify the most effective one. Note how changes in the pacing and the language make a difference in how others react.

Write a Poem

Like humor, poetry is an especially delicate type of writing—every sound, every word, every pause has the potential to tip the scale toward success or failure. So even if you're not a humorist or a poet, practicing with humor and poetry can be an excellent way to fine-tune your skills.

Read a few poems at the library or online at www. poets.org. Read a short, accessible introduction to the art like *The Poetry Home Repair Manual* by Ted Kooser or *A Poetry Handbook* by Mary Oliver. Then try your hand at it a few times.

Even if you don't take to the genre, even if poetry leaves you cold and your goal is to write science articles or medical thrillers, this exercise will give your prose a touch of lyricism that will make it even more enjoyable to read.

Block Crock

You need to focus on one genre.   Some people like to opine that you must dedicate yourself to poetry or the short story or the novel and refine it to perfection. But there are no electrified fences along the genre borders, and plenty of successful writers have crossed them. Even if you do want to stick to one genre, try playing around with the others. You just might discover something valuable.

Write a Mystery Story

In mystery, plot is essential. So try it, regardless of whether or not it's what you're interested in writing.

Imagine someone committing a crime, and figure out exactly how, where, when, and why they did it. Then imagine what they did to hide the evidence. Start your story with someone coming upon the crime scene, and follow that character as he or she tries to unravel what you as the author already know.

As you slowly determine what to reveal, when to reveal it, and how to reveal it, you gain plotting skills that serve your nonmystery writing. After all, what keeps people reading a mystery story or anything else is some form of suspense—a desire to know what happens next or what happened in the past that led to the current state of affairs.

Write a Human-Mystery Story

Our fellow human beings mystify us all the time. Next time you find yourself asking, *Why would someone do that?* write a story that attempts to answer your question. The act might be something awful or altruistic or just plain odd, but the important thing is to think up a set of circumstances, beliefs, or experiences that could possibly lead someone to do it—even if it's utterly inexplicable from your initial point of view.

Note that doing this doesn't mean you have to justify an act you find morally unacceptable—the decision your character makes might very well be utterly wrong and destructive. But in trying to solve the mystery of how it happened, you develop the ability to write about characters who do good, bad, and seemingly bizarre things in a realistic and believable way.

It's All in the Details

The phrase "concrete details" comes up in just about any creative writing class or book. But some writers still shy away from them. I do—and I'm pretty sure it's because, after reading some novels as a kid that opened with 5 or 10 tedious pages of description, I still fear boring my readers to death in a similar fashion. But it's all a matter of balance. Sprinkling details throughout your work—solid, five-senses details—makes it come alive and involves your reader much more deeply.

Write a scene—it doesn't need to have a plot or lead anywhere—in which you include at least one detail for each of the five senses. Make the coffee a character drinks lukewarm and milky. Make someone's high heels clack against the floor. Readers need something solid to grab on to so they can become immersed in the world in which your piece exists.

Remember, what makes a particular word or phrase important isn't just that it advances the plot or adds to your argument. It's also important to make the reader enjoy the experience of reading your work, so they actually finish it.

Edit Your Everyday Writing

Don't keep everyday, mundane writing tasks in a separate mental compartment away from your creative writing. Making an effort to keep your e-mails, letters, memos, or whatever else you dash out on a daily basis as clear, concise, and interesting as possible is a great way to fit in some extra training and become a better writer over time. (Of course, if your boss wants that memo out in an hour, you might want to refrain from doing 12 revisions.)

> **Block Crock**
>
> **This isn't *real* writing.** Even if it's not "art," any written communication offers you a chance to practice your skills—which will wind up making your "real" writing better.

Take a Paragraph Apart

And then put it back together. Does each sentence have a logical connection to the ones before and after it? Does the paragraph work as a whole, or does it go off on a tangent somewhere in the middle and need to be cut in half or edited? When you look at your paragraph as a part of the overall piece, does it make sense to pause before it and after it?

Respect Your Grammar

Don't fall into the trap of thinking that grammar is some sort of outdated concept that just holds true artists back and inhibits their bold, free-wheeling creativity. Like the aforementioned musician whose progress advanced by leaps and bounds after he started learning musical theory, a writer can gain a new level of control and skill by learning the basics of grammar.

Even if you have a natural feel for grammar, as many writers do, knowing the actual rules and terms that make up "writing theory" can give you the ability to do a lot of new tricks without muddling up your writing. Understanding grammar doesn't trap you—it frees you. Read *The Elements of Style* by Strunk and White and *Woe Is I* by Patricia T. O'Conner (they're both short).

Look for Chances to Practice

Are there ways you can volunteer your writing talents? Does a community organization need help putting out a newsletter? Does your house of worship want contributors for the weekly bulletin? Do you have a friend with a small business who could use your writing services?

The sheer act of writing, of putting words together and forming sentences, can be enough to get you back in the groove with your novel-in-progress.

Exercise: Master Your Art

A few years back, when I was finishing up a long round of therapy with a psychologist who had helped me finally triumph over a history of anxiety disorders and obsessive-compulsive behaviors, I happened to be a guest at a wedding where professional dancers had been hired. Their job was to get the party started and keep it going by mixing with the crowd and encouraging them to get up and boogie.

I watched as a young girl, perhaps 10 or 11, was approached by one of the female dancers, who escorted her out of the crowd on the sidelines and took her for a spin around the floor. The girl had a shy, awkward air and one of those faces that you could tell she would have to grow into—with the sort of strong, dramatic features that are startling on a 10-year-old, but would be strikingly beautiful by the time she turned 16.

She looked up at her dancing partner with stars in her eyes, self-conscious but clearly enthralled, and grateful for the help and attention. The dancer taught her some steps, they did some laughing and twirling, and when the song ended, the dancer moved on to her next customer as the girl, with clear regret, watched her walk away.

The scene riveted my attention for some unknown reason, and soon afterward I found myself writing about it with great emotion. It wasn't until later that I made the connection with what was going on in my own life—with my own "professional dancer."

 Breakthroughs

The greatest thing in style is to have a command of metaphor.

—Aristotle, *Poetics*

So although I emphasize hard work and practical strategies in this book and encourage a down-to-earth attitude to writing, I do have a deep appreciation of the very personal—and yes, sometimes perhaps mystical—part of the process. Craft is important, but so is what we commonly think of as "art."

There are things in our world and in our lives that are difficult to see without metaphors serving as a bridge. When I saw the link between the end of my therapy and the end of the dance, I was amazed that so much was going on in my writing that I wasn't even aware of. It would have been difficult for me to experience or express love and sympathy for myself directly (yes, even after all that therapy)—but I was able to see myself in the awkward little girl. And though I'd grown very attached to my therapist and was a little afraid of not having him to lean on anymore, watching the dancer move on—just doing her job—made me understand that our parting was a necessary sadness.

When you find writing difficult, it could be that you need to expand your artistic soul a little. If you feel that you're able to write but you just don't know what to write about, try some of the following ideas.

Open Your Heart and Mind

In Chapter 1, I talked about the figurative suits of armor we sometimes wear and how they can get in the way when we sit down to write. Sometimes a writer needs to tough out uncomfortable or even painful moments to discover truth and beauty. Casting aside prejudices, hostilities, and habitual ways of thinking and feeling can lead us to the kind of breakthroughs that take our art to a new level.

Today, be extra patient with someone who irritates the daylights out of you. Go out of your way to read or watch a commentator who you routinely disagree with—keeping your mouth shut and your mind open the whole time.

Allowing the world to flow through you, experiencing its complexities more fully, can transform your writing and lend it a new degree of depth and wisdom.

Open Your Eyes and Ears

Life offers us plenty of distractions, now more than ever. Next time you're on a train, look around and count how many people are plugged into various devices, focused on anything but the scene around them. I certainly indulge in books and music sometimes on the train, but I also try to reserve a few rides a week for just "being there." Because the fact is, even after years of daily commuting, there's always something new to see through the window, or in the next row of seats.

Block Crock

My life is boring—what could I possibly write about? If you think your life is boring, you're not paying attention. You're surrounded by pulsing life all the time: birth, death, conflict, desire, change. Even if you live alone in a tent in the middle of a forest, ants are doing amazing things right under your feet.

Beginning in childhood, we're told to stay focused—
on our textbook, on our task, on the head of the
child in front of us in line in the schoolyard. Stretch
your neck. Look around. Go to the nearest window,
look through it for 1 minute, and write about what
you see.

Wait

You're sitting at your keyboard or in front of your
notebook. You're ready. You want to write. But nothing's happening. You sigh. You tap your fingers. Your
heart rate starts going up. You feel a little sweaty.
You start thinking of other things to do. You start
thinking that you're a hopeless loser who should just
give it up ....

Stop. Rewind. How about giving yourself, oh, 5
minutes or so before you decide you're doomed?
Complex tasks require a little adjustment, a little
mental preparation. That's why it takes office workers a while to settle in at their desks in the morning.
They get coffee; they get comfortable; they arrange
things on their desks; they look at their calendars.
Then they ease into the work of the day. Give yourself the same chance to get started before throwing
your hands up in defeat.

Breakthroughs

> The strongest of all warriors are
> these two—Time and Patience.
>
> —Leo Tolstoy, *War and Peace*

Don't Be a Big Floating Head

Doing mental work—like writing—can lead us to neglect the physical side of life. But you don't want your writing to be completely abstract and detached from the physical world.

Keep some balance between your intellect and your body. Get your hands dirty. Take a yoga class. Do a home-improvement project. Not only do physical experiences lend sensual detail to your work, they can also break up the mental knots that can be a direct cause of writer's block.

> **Patience, Patience** _____
>
> It took Donna Tartt 10 years to publish _The Little Friend_, the follow-up to her hit 1992 novel _The Secret History_.

Make Connections

Metaphors and similes are essential tools of the creative writer, and they don't always come easily. Observation and contemplation are crucial. As you move through the world today, ask yourself again and again, _What does that remind me of?_ Ask it about a flower, a squirrel, an overflowing trash bin, a roomful of busy workers, a bus unloading its passengers.

Tomorrow, make a list of "things that are fast." Keep it in mind all day, noting everything that strikes you as fast. You'll be surprised at how many original, creative ways there are to express the concept of fast, and the next time you're describing something fast, you won't have to resort to a cliché, like "as fast as lightning."

Appreciate Your "Material"

Here's a great thing about being a writer: all that crappy stuff in your life—the failures, the sorrows, the embarrassing moments—are pure gold in writing terms. When you write about loss and rejection and all the other hard parts of life, you're making lemonade out of lemons, and more importantly, you're providing people with comfort, because they're dealing with the same stuff.

And if you simply can't bring yourself to admit that you once tripped and fell flat on your face while flirting with your seventh-grade crush, you can just make one of your characters do it. (That actually happened to ... er, someone I know.)

Read, Read, Read

Learn by example. Most writers love to read—it's what started them wanting to write in the first place—but as we get older and busier, we might slip out of the habit. To produce good writing, you need to consume good writing. Remember the saying: "Garbage in, garbage out." It was originated by computer programmers, but it applies to just about anything. Read book reviews and seek out things that pique your interest. Ask friends for recommendations. Browse the library or bookstore. Or just walk over to your bookshelf and pick up that book you've been "meaning to read" for the past 12 years or so. Rediscover the joy of reading, and bring a new sense of joy to your writing.

Breakthroughs

Life can't defeat a writer who is in love with writing, for life itself is a writer's lover unto death.

—Edna Ferber

The Least You Need to Know

- The best way to build your confidence is to build your skills.
- Trying different forms and genres can make you better at your own.
- Before you write, you have to read—and watch, and listen, and think, and maybe have a cup of coffee.

Daily Confidence Builders

In This Chapter

- Becoming more confident as a writer (and a person)
- The illusion of the "writer" identity
- Coping with criticism … *and* praise
- Putting writing in the proper perspective

Lack of confidence is a very common cause of writer's block. And it's not surprising. After all, when you take a step back and look at the big picture, you can't help wondering, *There are billions of people in the world … why would anyone want to listen to me?*

This chapter is dedicated to building your confidence as both a writer and a person. As Chapter 3 pointed out, competence is a crucial ingredient of confidence. Your confidence in yourself and your work will increase over time as you get better and better at what you do.

But there also comes a point when confidence requires a set of beliefs and a leap of faith. You can't sit at your desk working and working to become

The Best Writer Ever before you put your stuff out there. Where would the world be if writers did that? There wouldn't be much reading material available, that's for sure.

Writers *Write*

A lot of people—artists especially—have a tendency to think that "writer" (or "poet" or "musician" or whatever) is some sort of definable, fixed identity. What that definition is, they might not know exactly ... but they keep believing that it exists, and they keep chasing after it. They might think being a writer doesn't count unless you've actually published. They might have a vague notion that being a writer requires a certain level of devotion or commitment or a particular lifestyle. They might believe that artists are born, not made. Worse yet, there are plenty of critics around, amateur and professional alike, who insist on trying to separate the "real" writers and artists from their presumably inadequate brethren.

If you want to define *writer*, check the dictionary. My dictionary says a writer is "a person who writes."

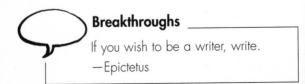

Breakthroughs

If you wish to be a writer, write.
—Epictetus

Don't waste a moment wondering if you're really a writer. If you get caught up in pondering that kind of nonsense, not only will your faith in yourself erode but you won't have any time left to write. Then you really *won't* be a writer.

Here are some more productive ways to pump up your self-confidence so you can concentrate on your drafts instead of your doubts.

All That You Are

What makes you—and for that matter, everyone else on Earth—qualified to be a writer is a unique perspective. No one else has your particular combination of genetics and environment and experience, so you bring something absolutely special to your writing that no one else can.

Don't believe me? Try this: make a list of some of the ingredients that add up to "you." Start with general things:

- Gender
- Nationality
- Religious background

Then move on to anything that's part of who you are:

- Vegetarian
- Former cheerleader
- Big brother
- Grandmother

- Cook
- Spanish speaker
- Piano player

You'll be amazed at how long the list gets, and it will remind you that you are, indeed, one precious snowflake.

Now, look again at your list and see if there aren't some less-flattering things you might have left out. This isn't a resumé—include the not-so-great stuff, too! It just might be that the parts of your life and identity that you're not so thrilled with (for example: I smoke a pack a day, I'm bad at telling jokes, my housekeeping habits are one step below Oscar Madison's) are the things that give you the best material.

Paul Feig has taken his memories of being a high-school outsider and turned them into two riotous, poignant memoirs (*Kick Me* and *Superstud*) as well as the TV cult hit *Freaks and Geeks*. Remember that what you reflexively think of as a weakness can often turn out to be a strength, so strive to be honest, not to make a flawless impression. Others may admire those who seem perfect—but they *like* those who seem human.

Hang Up Your Rejection Letters

Yes, put them right up there on your fridge or your bulletin board or the wall of your writing room. Look them square in the face. See them as a badge of honor. If you're a published writer and have some bad reviews, hang those up, too.

Rejection and criticism is something you have in common with even the most successful writers in the world. And as long as you write, no matter how accomplished you become, they'll continue to be a part of your life, so you might as well learn to deal with them now. It will make you strong.

Hang Up the Good Stuff, Too

Don't just include the bad stuff; you need to display the positive comments you get, too:

- Your creative writing class story with the B+ on it
- The complimentary e-mail your friend sent you after reading your poem
- The performance review that mentions your skill at composing memos
- Your feature that was published in the community newspaper
- Your award certificate from the sixth-grade essay contest

Being open to acceptance and praise is just as important as being open to rejection and criticism.

Don't Apologize for Being a Writer

Never, never do this. You don't need to apologize for being an unpublished writer, or an aspiring writer, or an amateur writer. *Ever.*

First of all, every professional writer started out as an unpublished, aspiring, amateur writer. (And plenty of them stayed that way for a long time.) Second, and more important, if you value your writing, it doesn't matter whether others do or not. Different individuals and communities value different things. If you're a high school student in Texas, you might get more applause for playing football than for writing. If you're in a convent, the other nuns might put more emphasis on helping the poor than composing a sonnet. Get your own values and priorities in order, and live your life accordingly. If they don't always match everyone else's values and priorities, there's no reason for you to apologize to them any more than there is for them to apologize to you.

> **Breakthroughs**
>
> While one person hesitates because he feels inferior, the other is busy making mistakes and becoming superior.
> —Henry C. Link

Consider Blogging

It's not for everyone, and it's far from a guaranteed route to print publication, but if nothing else, blogging or setting up a website can be an easy way for friends and family to read (and comment on) your latest work, which can nourish you and keep you going.

One of the things that can undermine our confidence is feeling self-conscious and needy when we press piles of paper into people's hands, asking them to spend their valuable time reading our stuff. E-mailing them a link with a "check it out if you have some time" note will make you feel more comfortable and make it easier for them as well.

Stop Worrying About Being a Hack

Do you fear that producing too much too fast will reveal you to the world as a so-called hack? Some people do have a prejudice against writers they regard as "too prolific." The presumption is that your work is shallow and rushed, and not enough pruning and primping and suffering has been put into it. Of course, it might also be that those people are blocked and unproductive and just hate it that you're not. And you don't want to subconsciously slow yourself down because of a fear of what others think.

If you're naturally prolific, be prolific. Go at your natural pace. The quality of your work is a separate issue from the speed at which it's produced.

Block Crock

How good can he be, churning out a new novel every year? Some people write faster; some people write slower. Follow your own pace, and don't compare yourself (negatively *or* positively) with other writers.

Read to Your Dog

Get used to the feeling of standing up and reading your work out loud. It might come in handy some-day when you're promoting your book ... and it's also a great way to build confidence in yourself and your material. As a bonus, reading your work out loud can help you hear its rhythms and identify what flows smoothly and what doesn't.

When you've become comfortable in front of the dog, move on to a good friend, and then work your way up to an informal group reading, taking turns with supportive friends in a relaxed environment. Don't forget the refreshments.

Know Who or What You're Writing For

In the words of Bob Dylan: "You gotta serve some-body." We find it much harder to be motivated when we're not clear on our ultimate purpose. And if you've always liked to write, all the way back to childhood, you might never have actually stopped and asked yourself what your purpose is. If you find yourself blocked as you grow older, it could be because you've lost touch with your sense of purpose.

Maybe your purpose is exactly the same as it was when you wrote as a child—to have fun, to work out your emotions, to get your thoughts in order, to sort through the mysteries of the world. Maybe as you've matured and changed, you have different or addi-tional goals: to make the world a better place or to share your expertise in a certain field. Maybe you're writing for Jesus, or for Truth, or for Beauty. Maybe you're making Art for Art's Sake. Maybe you have one particular person, real or imaginary, in mind when you write. Maybe you just want to tell good stories so people can escape into a fictional world and enjoy themselves for a few hours.

It's up to you to figure out what's important to you and what you want to accomplish, because if you don't have at least some sense of purpose, you'll probably find it difficult to keep going.

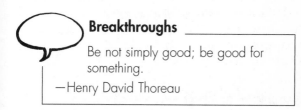

Breakthroughs

Be not simply good; be good for something.

—Henry David Thoreau

Know the Purpose of Each Piece

Aside from understanding your overall purpose, clarifying your intentions is an excellent way to help you through a specific episode of writer's block. Instead of working on your novel/poem/article/ speech, write a paragraph about what you want to accomplish with your novel/poem/article/speech. Clearing that up might suddenly make your task seem a whole lot easier.

Take a Class—Online or Off

It's easier nowadays than ever for writers to get professional advice and feedback. Writing programs have increased in number in the past couple decades, and options range from relatively inexpensive continuing-education classes at nearby colleges, to online classes offered by such groups as The Gotham Writer's Workshop, to low-residency graduate programs that allow you to do most of your work from home.

There are two big advantages to taking a class aside from what you actually learn in the course. One is structure, which forces you to produce on a regular basis. The other is the opportunity to be around other writers, who can not only share their reactions and thoughts about your work but also provide a sense of solidarity.

Block Crock

Those writing classes are full of dilettantes and no-talents. If someone's going to the effort and expense to take a class, he or she obviously takes writing fairly seriously. Don't use baseless excuses like this to avoid a writing class. Their purpose is to provide learning, structure, and community—not an arena where you get to judge your classmates (and they get to judge you).

Writing is a lonely pursuit, and feeling disconnected can lead to depression and writer's block—a particular risk for beginners who haven't yet had the chance to relate to an audience. It can seem intimidating at first, but once you gather up the

courage and try a class, it can be an extremely ben-
eficial and confidence-building experience.

Learn the Words of Strength

The Three Words of Strength: *I don't know*.

The Two Words of Strength: *I'm sorry*.

The One Word of Strength: *Thanks*.

These are things confident people say, and confident people make confident writers. People who are
afraid of seeming weak go out of their way to avoid
these statements. In the long run, it only makes
them weaker.

Admit when you don't know something. Nobody
knows everything, and other people like to feel
they have something to offer in a conversation, too.
They don't just want to be part of your audience.

When it comes to writing, an overly authoritative
voice can make you sound condescending, and iron-
ically, writers who want to appear too all-knowing
often wind up writing mushy, noncommittal prose
because they're afraid to make a mistake. Take
responsibility if you screw up—everyone messes up
from time to time. Even *The New York Times* has to
print corrections.

And never forget that there's no such thing as a
self-made man (or woman). Maintain a healthy and
generous sense of gratitude for those who've helped
along the way.

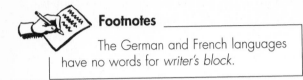

Footnotes

The German and French languages have no words for *writer's block*.

Get Some Perspective

Writer's block almost always involves some sort of distorted thinking. Getting past your misperceptions (whether they're about yourself, the nature of writing, the chances of success, or the market for your work) can go a long way toward calming anxieties and putting you back on the right track.

Let's consider some facts that can help you get a clearer and more realistic idea of what you're trying to accomplish—and break through some of the myths that might be stopping you.

It's Not Such a Long Shot

True, writing is a competitive business. It takes some hard work to make a living at it. But the same could be said for being a doctor. If you're haunted by the feeling that your chances are exceedingly slim, it's not surprising that you might feel unmotivated and stop trying.

It's important to remember that while, say, being a number-one *New York Times* best-selling author is indeed quite a long shot, being a published writer isn't. The number of new titles published annually is in the range of 175,000, and because of changes in technology, that number is rising, not falling. That's a lot of books, and somebody has to write them. Why not you?

Block Crock

Writing is just too competitive. I don't have a chance. True, there are a whole lot of aspiring writers out there, but there are also a whole lot of book publishers, magazines, newspapers, websites, journals, theater companies, TV shows, movie studios ….

Avoid poring over the 15 books on the best-seller list. Instead, take a look around at the teeming shelves of the nearest superstore. If your goal is to be published and read, it might still be a challenge—but it's not the impossible dream.

Writing Is Just Talking on Paper

Why should anyone listen to you? Well, why do they listen to you now when you talk? For that matter, why do we listen to people at all, in person or on the radio or TV? Writing is just another form of talking. Just because something's written down instead of spoken doesn't automatically make it any deeper or truer or more entertaining than something said out loud. It just makes it … written down. And also makes it easier for more people to "hear" it, now and in the future.

If you have things you believe are worth opening your mouth and saying—stories, jokes, opinions, whatever—then why would you think you have nothing worth writing? If the idea that you're "writing" intimidates you, remind yourself that you're just talking on paper, and jabber away. You can edit it later—which is another advantage writing has over talking.

Breakthroughs

Poets are born, not paid.

—Wilson Mizner

Writing Is Often a Part-Time Job

If you think having a day job means you're not a real success as a writer, think again. Most writers, including ones who get nice reviews and sell fairly well, still have to do other things to pay the bills. Some teach; some do more commercial kinds of writing, like ads or speeches or press releases; some work in bookstores and libraries; some do completely unrelated jobs—which can work out very nicely, as even the most hardworking writers often find it difficult to spend more than a few hours a day at it and like to keep a foot planted in the "real world" to get ideas and inspiration. (See the "The Unlived Life Is Not Worth Examining" section in Chapter 7.)

If you're a poet, count on a second career—like William Carlos Williams, who was a practicing doctor; or Wallace Stevens, a lawyer who composed poetry while commuting to his insurance company job every day; or Frank O'Hara, who manned the front desk at New York's Museum of Modern Art.

Patience, Patience

Henry Roth published his first novel, *Call It Sleep,* in 1934. He published his next—the first volume in the *Mercy of a Rude Stream* series—in 1994. That just might be the world record! (He did, however, get some short pieces done during that 60-year stretch, collected in the 1987 volume *Shifting Landscape.*)

It's Not *All* Connections

True, connections help. They've helped me—my background in the publishing world led to a fortunate connection that, years later, resulted in the chance to write my first book. But—also because of my background in the publishing world—I don't think for a minute that anyone would have let me write a book simply because of that connection. Publishers are way too interested in making money to do that kind of favor for anyone, and agents aren't going to put their reputation on the line by sending out anything their friends, families, and acquaintances ask them to. Now, maybe if there was a privately held company and the owner's beloved spouse had an itching to be the next Nora Roberts ... but those cases are extreme rarities.

Earlier in my career, I acquired and edited books, and I couldn't have gotten a friend's book published—unless I happened to have a friend who wrote a really great book. (Even then, there would have been no guarantees.) The system is set up in such a way that multiple approvals are needed for any major decision at a publishing house, so connections will take you only so far.

Do make some connections if you can—by taking classes, talking to teachers, joining writer's groups, or working in jobs that expose you to writers and books (or magazines, newspapers, TV, film, etc.) in some way, directly or indirectly. These will all be good for your career, even if they don't happen to land you a lucky big break.

But don't fall for the cynical cliché that you have to hobnob with the literary elite in New York to get anywhere. Connections might get you a reading you wouldn't otherwise have gotten, but they're not likely to get you a signed contract.

You Don't Know the Value of Your Writing

But your reader does. And it's as mysterious and unpredictable a thing as a spark of attraction between two people. What you think of as just another sentence or idea can be the sentence or idea that inspires, enlightens, shifts perspective, or otherwise changes a reader's life. You might find a way to say something that suddenly allows a concept to click in a reader's brain. You might move them to tears or laughter at moments you weren't trying to, because your words hit them in just the right place at the right time.

And those magic moments don't always come in the expected places, the classics or "important" books. We readers hungrily devour millions of words, because we never know where we're going to strike gold. It could be in a poem, a self-help book, or a science textbook. It could be in an old movie or on a scrap of paper in a fortune cookie. So don't decide what the reader will think or feel, or try too hard to anticipate your effect. Just write and let the magic happen by itself.

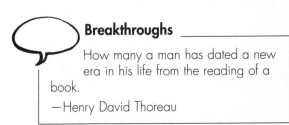

Breakthroughs

How many a man has dated a new era in his life from the reading of a book.

—Henry David Thoreau

You Don't Have to Be Mainstream to Make It

A phenomenon known as the "long tail" has emerged in the book business—and other art and entertainment fields—in recent years. First defined by Chris Anderson, editor of *Wired* magazine, it identifies the far end of the sales curve—the "long tail"—where more specialized, unusual, or niche items sell in much smaller quantities than the big, mainstream best-sellers in the middle of the curve. The thing is, a bunch of niche books can, cumulatively, sell more than the big best-seller (and can be more profitable for publishers, in these times when advances for big best-sellers can run into seven figures).

The development of the long tail has a lot to do with technologies that make writing, producing, and selling books easier and cheaper than ever, and what it means for you as an artist is that you can pursue your passion—and still find a place in the market. In the old days, many bemoaned the "death of the mid list," fearing that publishers would bother less and less with the lower-profile books that sold respectable but not blockbuster numbers. In fact, it seems that the opposite is occurring.

The web helps get the word out to the right audience for quirky or special-interest publications, and some writers make the leap to print publishing after building an established following online.

Despite this, you'll still hear some writers asserting that you have to "dumb down" your writing or write in only certain types of "hot" categories to sell. Don't listen to them.

Consider Self-Publishing

Sometimes the DIY approach is the right one, if you believe in your book, have the resources, and are willing to risk them—or if you just want to get it out there and get it read.

But don't kid yourself: only a very small percentage of self-published books are ever picked up by traditional publishers. Even with print-on-demand

technology making self-publication far more afford-
able than it used to be, making a profit is very
tough. And when you self-publish, the burden is
on you. No teams of professionals are there to help
you edit, proofread, design, promote, and sell your
book, like you would have with a publishing company that shares a financial interest in the project.
Reviewers and sales outlets approach self-published
books with more caution, because their contents
have not been vetted for accuracy and quality by
anyone other than the author.

Block Crock

Only losers self-publish.   That's
right—"losers" like Terry McMillan, Laurie
Notaro, Pat Conroy, Nikki Giovanni,
Mark Twain, Ernest Hemingway, and
E. Lynn Harris. And "losers" like the authors
of mega-sellers *The One-Minute Manager,
The Artist's Way, The Joy of Cooking, The
Christmas Box, What to Expect When
You're Expecting, What Color Is Your
Parachute?, In Search of Excellence, Life's
Little Instruction Book,* and *When I Am an
Old Woman I Shall Wear Purple.*

But if you simply want actual books on hand to sell
(or give) to anyone who's interested, and find the traditional publishing process frustrating and discouraging, self-publishing with a well-established company
is an alternative worth considering. After all, America
was founded on that kind of initiative—Thomas

Paine self-published his pamphlet *Common Sense*, sold half a million copies, and helped inspire the war for independence!

Yes, some people will still automatically look down their nose at any self-published book, but those people are mostly in the publishing industry. Your average reader does not care whether the spine says "Random House" or "Joe Blow Press." She just wants the book to be good.

You're Not Doing It for the Money, Anyway

Are you? If you're doing it for money, you're better off getting an accounting or law degree or learning how to fix cars or computers. Writing can pay, but, simply put, there are much more reliable ways to get a healthy, steady income.

Breakthroughs

The profession of book writing makes horse racing seem like a solid, stable business.

—John Steinbeck

You write, most likely, because you enjoy it, and that's a very good reason—maybe the best reason of all. Never lose touch with the nonfinancial rewards of writing, whether it's the sheer excitement of creating, the happiness at seeing someone enjoy or benefit from what you've written, or the simple satisfaction of expressing yourself and communicating with others. I'm delighted to get paid for my work, of course, but the pieces of writing that have meant the most to me over the years had nothing to do with a paycheck, including a eulogy for a close family member, a couple of personal letters, some silly stuff that made people laugh—and pretty much all my poetry. I'd rather make my money digging ditches and be able to write what I want than turn my writing into "just a job." And that's a perspective that's kept me writing year after year after year ... paycheck or no paycheck.

The Least You Need to Know

- Writing requires hard work, but also a little faith.
- All it takes to "be a writer" is to write.
- Rejection and criticism are part of *every* writer's life.
- Never forget the things that matter most— and never define success only in monetary terms.

Take Your Time

In This Chapter

- Setting your priorities
- Grabbing every chance to write
- Lifestyle changes and smart time-management equal more time and energy for writing

The picture of "writer's block" that usually comes to mind in our collective imagination is of someone sitting woefully at his desk with a wastebasket overflowing with crumpled drafts at his side. But a more accurate image in many cases would be of an empty chair—because someone has never actually sat down to start writing in the first place.

If that's your situation, it could very well be that you're not so much blocked from writing but blocked from *finding the time*—or more likely, making the time. That can seem like the hardest part, especially when you have constant demands on your schedule.

In the first part of this chapter, I look at ways to fit writing into your life that you may be overlooking. In the second part, I go over habits you can eliminate or reduce to free up more time for writing.

Windows of Opportunity

You might, like me, dream of traveling the world for months at a time, writing at sidewalk cafés and at the antique desk in your lovely *pensione*. Or spending the entire summer in a beachside cottage, scribbling away on your deck chair as the waves wash ashore in the background. Unfortunately, you might also, like me, not be independently wealthy. But there is hope.

If you took the advice in Chapter 2 and you've now got notebooks, notebooks everywhere, you can discover chances to squeeze in some writing at all sorts of unexpected times and places. Consider some of these, and even if you take advantage of only a few of them, you'll see an increase in productivity.

> **Breakthroughs**
>
> The ultimate of being successful is the luxury of giving yourself the time to do what you want to do.
>
> —Leontyne Price

Your Commute

Mass transit—it's good for the environment, and good for your writing. If mass transit is available to you, leave the car at home and use it. You'll be adding a nice chunk of time to your day in which you can read, think of ideas, ... and write.

It's not just actual traveling time that offers you a writing opportunity. It's also the waiting time at the train station ... or the bus stop ... or the airport. Find a quiet corner and go to it—but you might want to set your watch alarm in case you get so deep into the zone that you risk missing the P.A. announcements.

Lunchtime

Your cafeteria buddies will be likely to understand if you ditch them once or twice a week to go somewhere quiet and work on your latest short story. (Maybe they'll even agree to read it when you're done.) And if you're one of those people who work through lunch, do your best to give up that habit, unless your job security truly depends on it and you have no choice for the time being.

Take your lunch hour. You'll be more motivated and energetic getting through the afternoon if you have that great feeling of having gotten some writing done, and it will remind you that there's more to life than your job. Plus, you can get something healthier for your midday meal than cookies from the vending machine.

While You Wait ...

It's the upside of overbooked doctors: the gift of time. Take out your notebook in the waiting room.

Same for appointments with lawyers, clients, personnel directors, mechanics, bankers, and anyone else who's running behind schedule today.

Block Crock

I need a day off or a free weekend so I can get some writing done. Someone once pointed out that if you write a page a day, at the end of a year you can have a 365-page novel finished. When your busy life doesn't seem to allow for creative time, remember that short writing sessions here and there add up fast—and that if you keep waiting for the just-right opportunity before you pick up your pen, you'll squander them.

And it's not just while you're waiting for your appointment. Fit in writing in other seemingly wasted spots of time, like …

Write while you're under the dryer at the hairdresser. And while you're there, consider getting a low-maintenance haircut that doesn't require an hour and a half of blow drying, gelling, and other upkeep every week.

Write at the gym during the 90-second rest period during weight-lifting sets. It will be interesting to see what you come up with when you're pumped.

Write at the drugstore while you wait for your pre-scription to be filled. I guarantee it'll be much more fun than taking yet another tour of the shampoo aisle!

Write while you wait in the seemingly never-ending lines at the department of motor vehicles. You might actually finish that epic trilogy.

During a Party

Stuck at a big social event where you hardly know anyone and you're about to take your third trip to the buffet table just to pass the time? Sneak off with your notebook and find a hiding place for 20 minutes. For all anyone knows, you were in the restroom.

On a Sick Day

Nap, get plenty of fluids, and write. It's more pro-ductive than watching the soaps, and being sick might even give you some material for a brooding, powerful novel about a character coming face to face with her own mortality. Or a limerick about Kleenex.

Breakthroughs

Great ideas are often born on a street corner or in a restaurant's revolving door.

—Albert Camus

On Vacation

Whether you're relaxing in your dream beachside cottage, taking a break while the kids splash in the pool, or sitting on the hotel balcony, you can write while you're on vacation. When your spouse is driving and you're not responsible for studying the map and telling him or her where to turn, pick up your pen and write. Some lovely scenery you drive by could inspire some equally lovely writing.

Even if you don't go anywhere, you could use some of your paid vacation time, if you have it, for writing. It can be just as much of a relaxing escape as a Caribbean island, especially if you turn off the phone and order in your meals.

Breakthroughs

All the really good ideas I ever had came to me while I was milking a cow.

—Grant Wood

If You Have Kids

If you're trying to write and be a parent at the same time—especially in those early years when kids need pretty much around-the-clock attention—you've got a challenge on your hands. Whether you're staying at home, going to work, or doing a bit of both, your time is going to be pretty restricted.

This might simply be a period in your life when your writing productivity will be lower, as well it should be, as you've got some extremely important other work to do. Most writers, even pros, have to work around other obligations and other kinds of employment to fit writing in. And what's a bigger obligation or more demanding kind of employment than parenthood?

It's not always possible to spend as much time writing as you'd like. (That's true for everyone, not just new moms and dads.) But when you do get a rare, precious break, you won't want to fritter it away with a case of writer's block, so keep reading and don't give up completely!

Block Crock

I'm not going to be able to write again until the kids are in college.   You might get less writing done while you're raising kids, but with a little inventiveness, you can sneak it in here and there. Try writing some bedtime stories for them—or *with* them.

One option: choose something else to neglect instead of your creative impulses. If the kids are sleeping or with a sitter, don't use the time to go to a movie, polish the furniture, or get your hair done. Use it to write, if only for an hour or so. When you're picking them up from school, stay in the car and write instead of hanging out and chatting with the other parents. And when you just can't manage a spare moment, forget about writing and enjoy this once-in-a-lifetime chance to nurture your little ones and be the most important person in the world to them. They're the ones who'll love you whether you win a Pulitzer or not.

Write Without Ceasing

The apostle Paul advised his fellow Christians to "pray without ceasing." How is that possible? Well, if you think of prayer as an attitude or way of being—something that is a part of your outlook, your values, your whole life—you can apply the same principle to writing.

It's not just the physical, formal act of writing that's important; it's the observing, the absorbing, the mental processing, the experiencing. Don't think of time away from your keyboard as time "not writing." Think of it as part of the process of *being* a writer ... all day, every day, without ceasing.

Time-Wasters to Avoid

If you truly want to write, and if you're committed to it, you might need to put some hard thought into your priorities—and decide whether you've got them in order.

Start looking at your time the way you look at your money. I expect you carefully consider what's worth your money and what's not. At the very least you probably keep track of it and guard it from those who might steal it. How about doing the same with something even more valuable: your time? Money is a renewable resource; time is not.

If you think you never have enough time to write, consider honestly what you *do* seem to have time for.

Flipping through celebrity magazines? Watching that *Seinfeld* rerun for the fourth time? Window-shopping? Playing *Tetris*? Attending social functions you don't particularly enjoy? If writing is more valuable to you than any of those things, why are you spending time on them instead of on writing? What might seem like a case of writer's block can in fact be a case of exhaustion. If you want writing to be part of your life, you have to make a conscious effort to conserve time and energy for it and give up some things that are less important to you.

Patience, Patience

The number of years between Thomas Pynchon's first and second novels: 3. The number of years between his third and fourth: 17.

Here are some guidelines for cutting down on various time- and energy-suckers ... and giving your creativity more room to grow.

Do a Time-Study

Managers and consultants look closely at how businesses operate to see where time is being wasted or not used as efficiently as possible. Do the same thing for yourself.

Keep a piece of paper handy for a week and record exactly what you spend your time doing. Did you run to the store for last-minute dinner ingredients three times when you could have thought ahead and made one trip? Did you put off folding the laundry and then wind up having to iron because stuff got wrinkled sitting in a jumble on the dresser? Did you get sucked in by an 8-hour *Twilight Zone* marathon? Did you spend 30 minutes in line at the supermarket because you went on Saturday afternoon instead of during the less-busy off-hours?

If potential writing time is slipping through your hands every day, it might be advisable to draw up a time budget and stick to it.

Unplug

The fact that most of us do our writing on computers these days certainly leads us into temptation, as it's so easy to drift out of that word-processing program and wind up at a shopping site or a poker site or a million other potential distractions. (*I'll just take a little break and see what's new on CNN.com … oh, this nine-page retrospective on the life of Elvis looks interesting!*)

Establish some rules such as the following to safeguard your time and ensure that your devices serve your purposes rather than running your life:

- Check personal e-mail no more than twice a day.
- If for some reason you absolutely must keep your e-mail program open while you write, turn off the sound so it doesn't ding every time a message arrives.

- Shut off the cell phone during your evening walk or when you're grabbing a bite at the diner.

- Set a kitchen timer when you're about to surf the net so you don't lose track and spend more time online than you planned.

- Leave the iPod at home at least 2 days a week and write during your commute instead.

- Don't log on during writing breaks—get away from the computer and don't come back until you're ready to start writing again.

- Make the most of one brilliantly useful piece of technology—the answering machine—by screening your calls and returning them only when it's convenient for you.

Learn to Say No

There's a reason this chapter is called "Take Your Time." It's *your time*—and you have to *take* it, not give it to others constantly, if you want to spend it writing. It's amazing how some people who wouldn't dream of asking for $20 from your wallet have no compunction about practically demanding the precious hours of your day.

Read up on assertiveness training, and limit your "yeses" to friends who truly need a favor, tasks that family members can't do for themselves, and social activities that will revitalize you, not make you feel drained and exhausted from fake-smiling.

Block Crock

I have so many other responsibilities. Be sure you distinguish between real responsibilities and favors done out of reflexive guilt. Driving your elderly mom to the doctor's office is not in the same league with baking 400 cookies for the annual bowling league party. Let them eat cake … from a bakery!

Create, Don't Consume

Shopping used to be about needing something and going out to find it. Now, far too often, it's about going out and trying to find something, anything, you can buy, whether you need it or not. The reasons for that are complex and beyond the scope of this book, but suffice it to say, many powerful societal forces strongly encourage you every day to *consume*, but encouragement to *create* is in relatively short supply. So consuming becomes a habit, a leisure activity, a default when there's supposedly nothing else to do ("let's hang out at the mall"). That's why many of us wind up with clothes we never wear clogging our closets, gadgets we never use hogging our cabinet space, and credit card balances that keep us enslaved to jobs we don't like for years—thus making it difficult to pursue our dreams, like writing.

You do have the power to resist—and when you do, you'll find that the satisfaction of buying yet another sweater or DVD or pair of earrings pales in comparison to the satisfaction of creating something yourself. Try these techniques to consume less and create more:

Schedule twice-yearly trips to the mall, and bring a list of things you need: school clothes for the kids, a new lamp to replace the broken one, whatever. While you're there, pick up the next 6 months' worth of birthday and holiday gifts, and the cards and wrapping paper to go with them.

For other necessary purchases, go to a nearby specialty store that's not part of a mall, or pick them up during your lunch hour so you'll have to get back to work and won't have time to linger and do habitual, purposeless shopping.

Buy online—but don't browse there. Doing the former is a big time-saver; doing the latter is a big time-waster.

Each weekend, clean out another room in your house or apartment. Throw out or donate anything that's just taking up space. Think hard about how much time and money you spent accumulating this stuff ... and how much it really added to your happiness.

If you want to shop "just for fun" occasionally, do it at garage sales, flea markets, and thrift or vintage shops, where you're much more likely to find something truly special—and truly cheap. (Plus, there's something in the atmosphere of those kinds of history-filled places that inspires more creativity than sterile mall displays do.)

Beware of "Writing-Related Activity"

I'm glad you're reading this book, and I hope it's providing you with some practical advice and guidance to get you past your blocks. But I'd rather you put a bookmark in it and toss it on the shelf if it means you'll sit down right this minute and start writing.

Hundreds of valuable books, magazines, and websites are available to writers, but they can turn into a hindrance rather than a help if you make them a too-frequent habit and use them to postpone your confrontation with the blank page. I've been there myself, and it goes something like this: *I really want to write. I haven't done anything in so long. I've got to get back to writing. I think I'll go to the bookstore and browse through the writing section to get me in the mood.*

Try this instead: in between each chapter of this book, take a break and write a page. You might get so caught up in your writing project that you don't even need to come back and finish reading!

> **Breakthroughs**
>
> Planning to write is not writing. Outlining ... researching ... talking to people about what you're doing, none of that is writing. Writing is writing.
>
> —E. L. Doctorow

Clock Out

If your nonpaying (or less-paying) job—writing— constantly takes a backseat to your paying job, you're not going to have much energy left over at the end of the day to produce some pages.

If you have a firm schedule at work, you can leave it behind when your shift is over and turn your attention to other important things in your life. But if you're self-employed, or in a salaried position where the hours are a little more nebulous, it's up to you to set limits. Weigh your financial needs and wants, and your career ambitions, against your desire to write. Then commit your time accordingly.

As I pointed out in Chapter 4, many accomplished writers hold down other jobs—but they don't spend 60 or 70 hours a week at them if they want to get any writing done.

Patience, Patience

Peter Hedges' highly acclaimed debut novel, *What's Eating Gilbert Grape*, was followed—6½ years later, in 1998—by *An Ocean in Iowa*. He has gotten some other writing done, including an original and an adapted screenplay, but as of this writing, fans are still waiting for the next novel. Waiting and waiting and waiting ....

Exercise, Don't *Extra-Cise*

It's been noted with amusement that many of us take the elevator up to our offices and back down ... and then head to an expensive gym where we climb fake stairs to lose weight. Get off the treadmill (literally), and integrate exercise into your life.

Combine socializing with exercising by setting up a tennis date or a basketball game with friends. Walk or bike to nearby destinations, take the stairs, or do some housework and yard work. I'm not recommending that you stop exercising, just that you go about it in a more time-wise way. If you spend 2 or 3 fewer hours a week driving to and from the health club, changing into exercise clothes, and climbing up fake stairs, you'll have more time to write … and your house and yard will look better, too.

> **Breakthroughs**
>
> I write when I'm inspired, and I see to it that I'm inspired at nine o'clock every morning.
> —Peter De Vries

The Least You Need to Know

- When you actually start writing, it gets a lot easier.
- Thinking, dreaming, and watching the world—these are parts of the writing process, too, but actual writing is required for the words to wind up on the paper.
- Instead of waiting for a free day, take advantage of free hours—and even free minutes.
- If writing is truly your priority, you have to move it ahead of other things on your to-do list.

Chapter 6

Go Deep

In This Chapter

- When writer's block is a symptom of something else
- Tips for overcoming negative thinking and anxiety
- Why perfectionism is bad for art
- Exercises to mine buried treasure

The best writing tends to come from those who are willing to go deep—to follow thoughts, emotions, imagination, and logic to another level. By doing this, these writers offer us perspectives, possibilities, and insights we might never have been able to grasp through our own observation. They force us to slow down and immerse ourselves, rather than rush around and miss the details. They help us understand ourselves and our world by taking the time to put things under a microscope so we can see them in ways we never saw them before.

Sometimes writer's block needs the same kind of attention. If you've addressed the tasks in the previous chapters—setting up a comfortable writing space, building up your skill and confidence, managing your time—but still feel like there's something in the way, you might need to go deep to identify and break through whatever is holding you back. Learning how to take that plunge not only helps you get past your own emotional and psychological obstacles; it also enriches your creative and analytical abilities in the process.

In this chapter, we look at ways that deep-down personal issues can trip you up in your writing career and also how exploring the depths can take your writing to new heights.

What Trips You Up?

By the time you're old enough to hold a pen, your head is already packed with beliefs and ideas. Unfortunately, not all of them are quite accurate. Just think of some of the brilliant deductions you made as a child. For example, when I learned my mother would be bringing home a new baby from the hospital, I reached the obvious conclusion that a hospital was a kind of supermarket where babies were lined up on shelves, awaiting purchase. That particular misperception was cleared up just a few years later, but other similarly bright ideas I came up with during my childhood took a lot longer to straighten out.

Without remotely realizing it, you may have absorbed a lot of wrong information through the years. You might have also learned certain habits or outlooks that are not serving you well now. In many of us, these things become so embedded, so much a part of the way we think and act, that we don't always see them for the problems they are. We might even think they're *good* for us. But these deep-down issues can be insidious and have far-reaching effects on your happiness, your life—and yes, your writing success.

Breakthroughs

The most beautiful thing we can experience is the mysterious. It is the source of all true art and science.
—Albert Einstein

Do you recognize any of the following as possible causes of your writer's block?

- Procrastination
- Depression
- Perfectionism
- Anxiety and fear

Even if you don't recognize them as troublemakers just yet, consider whether some of these problems might be playing a role in your writer's block. In the following sections, I offer some suggestions for overcoming them.

Procrastination

Do you put off a lot of things, or is writing the only thing in your life that never seems to get done? Is the "block" chronic, or sudden and unusual? Remember that people don't just procrastinate when it comes to unpleasant tasks—sometimes they even put off things that make them feel happy, excited, or hopeful, because the prospect of feeling that way makes them nervous, or because they've developed the habit of "saving" good things for later, whether it's dessert, a good night's sleep, or the joy of writing.

Patience, Patience

Charles Frazier followed his smash best-seller and award-winner *Cold Mountain* with *Thirteen Moons*—a decade later.

If your writer's block fits in with an overall pattern of leaving things until the last minute, take heart. There are techniques to cure you of procrastination, and they will likely cure your block at the same time. Not only that, but you'll no longer have to endure those long post office lines on tax day. Try some—or all—of the following suggestions.

Break Up Big Tasks into Little Ones

Paradoxically, the more gigantic and overwhelming a task seems, and the more time we actually need for it, the more we tend to put it off. So don't think about completing your Great American Novel. Just think about completing your Great American

Chapter ... or for that matter, your Great American Paragraph. In fact, forbid yourself, at least for the first few weeks, from writing more than a half hour or an hour per day. If you know you must stop soon, you're more likely to start.

Picture It ...

Picture yourself a week from now having completed five more pages. Now picture yourself a week from now *not* having completed five more pages. Which feels better?

Make a List

Making a list helps me stay organized. Your list shouldn't include more than 5 to 10 items or it will defeat the purpose of the exercise. This list will help you focus on what you want to do, and it just might get you hooked on the satisfaction of drawing a big checkmark over each item when you complete it. As for what the items are, they can be small, individual writing jobs you need to complete for work, school, or personal reasons over the next month. Or they can be little steps in a single creative project, a sort of bare-bones outline:

1. Describe the main characters, Mary and John.

2. Show Mary and John having an argument about where to put their new TV.

3. Introduce Mary's mother, who calls on the phone or drops by during the argument.

4. Show Mary's mother putting her two cents in.

5. Describe John storming out of the house and heading for the bar to watch TV there.

Sure, you might want to do a little more fleshing out of your characters and plot afterward, but you'll have those bones solidly in place first—and that makes it a lot easier for your story to stand up instead of collapsing in a heap.

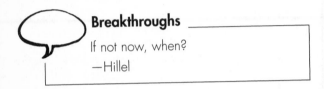

Breakthroughs

If not now, when?

—Hillel

Learn to Tell Time

Yes, yes, I know you've likely been doing it for years, but beyond being able to read the 3:20 on the face of a clock, you need to know how to add, subtract, and divide time. (Multiplying time, sadly, is not possible.)

Here's an example of what I'm talking about: if you need your story finished by 2 P.M. on Thursday so you can hand it in at class or make a submission deadline, and it's now 3:20 P.M. on Wednesday, you've got 22 hours and 40 minutes to get that done. Now, let's look at how fast time really flies!

- Lop off 7 or 8 hours in there for sleep, showering, eating breakfast, and that sort of thing.

- You've agreed to cover for your co-worker tomorrow morning for a couple hours while he goes to the dentist. Hmmm. There goes some more time.

- If you can submit electronically, you're ahead of the game—but if you'll need to print out or make extra copies of your work, subtract some time for that ... and remember that printers and photocopiers jam on a semi-regular basis. Factor in an extra 10 minutes there to be safe.

- Now ... why did you agree to that poker game tonight? Looks like your available time has slipped out of your hands once again.

When you add up the bits and pieces of time that are left, it grows heart-racingly clear that you're back on Last-Minute Lane, where all the traffic is moving much too fast and there's always a wee bit of road rage. Gasping for breath, pens and books tumbling out of your hands as you trip up the steps, you finally hand it in. Or do you ...?

Guess what: even if you *do* run this marathon all the time and it's been nothing but successful so far, there are questions to consider:

- How long do you think it might be before your luck runs out, especially considering that you're really stacking the odds against yourself?

- Do you think you're doing your best work under these circumstances?

- Do you want to keep living this way?

If you get a thrill out of beating the clock, pick up a game of *Scattergories* at the toy store. It comes with a nice loud buzzer, and because it's a word game, it's even good for your writing. But when you're doing something important to you, like trying to succeed in your chosen field, make time your friend, not your enemy. Get to know it and understand it. Listen to it tick. Feel what a minute is *really* like. Discover how much can be accomplished at a normal pace in the course of an hour.

I know there's a buzz that comes with pulling something off at the last moment—but as with other things that provide a buzz, a lot of downsides are attached, too, and those eventually outweigh the initial pleasure.

Block Crock

I do my best work under pressure.
A little deadline pressure can help you produce, but repeated last-minute stress, rushing, and panic don't tend to improve the quality of your work. Leave yourself a little extra time to read and revise—and breathe—and you're likely to see a distinct difference in the final product.

Depression

Depression isn't always as recognizable as you might expect. Even if you're aware that sudden changes in appetite and sleep habits, a lack of energy, or feelings of guilt and worthlessness are symptoms of depression, you might not know that there's also a type of chronic, low-level depression that affects many people in a less-noticeable, yet dramatic way. Very often it's the result of habitual negative thinking, filled with what psychologists call *cognitive errors*—illogical tendencies that color our thoughts, and as a result, affect the way we feel and act. Some forms of depression require professional treatment, but whether that's the case or not, anyone can benefit from learning some of these errors and working to avoid them. Here are a few common cognitive errors that might be contributing to your writer's block.

Disqualifying the Positive

Disqualifying the positive is what we do when we notice, remember, and give credence to every bit of bad feedback, but dismiss good feedback. Ask yourself how many times you've been complimented on your writing and immediately thought to yourself, *He's just being nice* or *She doesn't really know much about writing*. Why is it that you don't respond to negative criticism with *He's just being mean* or *She doesn't really know much about writing?*

Make an effort to treat all feedback—good, bad, and mixed—with the same degree of objectivity, asking yourself whether you honestly agree with it or not. It's easier at first to do this with written feedback, because you have more time to think clearly and form a logical reaction, but if you practice, you'll be able to do it in response to any feedback—whether you're receiving a standing ovation or being pelted with tomatoes.

Making It Personal

Personalization is the tendency to think it's all about you. Again, it's a natural tendency—we're all living smack in the middle of our own universe, after all. But this error can lead to major misinterpretations of what's going on around you. You've probably, at one time or another, been convinced that someone was mad at you and then found out later he was just in a bad mood and it had nothing to do with you. As writers, we're often very anxious to find out what people think of our work, and as a result, we might be watching a little too closely and thinking a little too much.

It's important to take a step back and remember that when we see things only from our own perspective, we're missing a multitude of alternative angles. If you give someone your story to read and it takes her longer to get to it than you expected, consider the possibility that she's just busy. If someone yawns while he's reading your story, consider that he might not have gotten enough sleep last night. If someone dislikes your story, consider that your writing style is not to her individual taste, or that she just doesn't like the genre you're working in, or that one of your characters reminded her of someone she can't stand and she couldn't see past that to assess your story on its own merits.

Now if she explains that it wasn't suspenseful enough or that she found a particular plot twist hard to believe, that might be valuable. But if you're just overinterpreting every frown, grimace, and twitch, you'll only drive yourself bananas.

Block Crock

He didn't laugh, so my humor piece is not funny.   Maybe it's not funny. Or maybe he's in a lousy mood. Or maybe he has no sense of humor. Or maybe his sense of humor isn't the same as yours. Or maybe his beloved grandmother just died. Or maybe he's afraid he has spinach between his teeth.

Getting Emotional

Emotional reasoning happens when we presume that our feelings are evidence of our immediate reality. That's simply not always the case. Consider someone who's terrified of ants—does it follow that ants are terrifying? Yet we frequently conclude that, for example, if we feel angry, someone has done us wrong. Or that if we feel sad, we must be in an awful situation. Our emotions are like feelers on a blind fish in the dark depths. They give us clues to our situation and surroundings, but they're definitely not enough to let us see the whole picture. They need light shed on them before we can accurately understand them. Our "feelers" might think we've run into a shark when in actuality we've only bumped into a guppy.

If you happen to get hit by a wave of sadness or anxiety while you're sitting at your writing desk, you might deduce that your feelings have something to do with writing: *I'm sad because I have no talent. I'm nervous because I know I'm not up to the task of writing a novel.* Start shining light on your emotional reactions, and you might discover that you're actually sad because you found out this morning that a friend is moving away and you were in too much of a rush to absorb the news at the time. Or maybe you're anxious because the presentation you have to make at the office next week is in the back of your mind.

It might turn out that your emotions do have to do with your writing, but if you don't take the time to analyze them, they will be a roadblock that stops you rather than a road sign that guides you. Incorporate your emotions with your logic instead of jumping to conclusions, and you'll find them surprisingly helpful. And if you've internalized the popular myth that writers are supposed to be depressed, forget it. Being depressed involves emotional numbness, exhaustion, distorted thinking, and loss of interest in the world. Do those sound like the makings of a great writer?

Breakthroughs

You don't have to suffer to be a poet. Adolescence is enough suffering for anyone.

—John Ciardi

Perfectionism

As David Burns, M.D., points out in his book *Feeling Good,* "if you are a perfectionist, you are guaranteed to be a loser in whatever you do." The quest for so-called perfection has derailed many on the path to their goals, and it's especially frustrating and damaging for writers, or artists of any kind. After all, art is subjective. You can get 100 percent on a spelling test or meet 100 percent of your sales target, but how do you score 100 percent on a novel, poem, or essay? Art can't be mass-produced, put together on an assembly line, and quality-tested. As another prominent psychologist, Carl Rogers, noted, "The very essence of the creative is its novelty, and hence we have no standard by which to judge it."

You need a willingness to take risks to create something new, and perfectionism discourages risks, because with risks come mistakes and failures as well as triumphs. Writers afflicted with perfectionism might find themselves petering out after what seems like a promising start, feeling that the project is not "coming out right"—or they might find it difficult to get started at all. If they do finish something, they're likely to do excruciatingly excessive editing or simply put it in a drawer, thinking it's not good enough for others to read.

If you have these tendencies, try some of the following techniques for overcoming perfectionism:

Spend an afternoon reading book reviews. Notice how the same exact book can get raves from some people and slams from others. What does that tell you about the quality or value of the book?

Keep in mind that art is an interaction between the artist and the audience. Each audience member is unique and brings something different to the interaction.

Therefore, as the old saying goes, you can't please all the people all the time.

> **Breakthroughs**
>
> Once you accept the fact that you're not perfect, then you develop some confidence.
>
> —Rosalynn Carter

Avoid all-or-nothing thinking. This is another "cognitive error," like the ones discussed in the earlier section on depression. And it's a widespread error—just look at the thumbs-up/thumbs-down, who's-hot/who's-not gimmicks that permeate pop culture. It's natural that we want things to be clear-cut, but reality rarely cooperates. No matter what the current issue of *Celebrity Worship Weekly* says, some portion of the population will find so-and-so "cool" and others won't. Most of what you experience will have good parts and not-so-good parts, and the same is true of what you produce.

Be aware that trying to seem perfect will, in the long run, only make you seem weak. Admitting mistakes and learning from them is a sign of strength. Anyone who looks down on you for admitting you made a mistake has his or her own learning to do.

When it comes down to the wire and you're about to quit yet again because "it's not good enough," ask yourself this: what's better, flawed art or no art?

Block Crock _____

I refuse to settle for inferior results.   So you're happier with no results?

Anxiety and Fear

Sometimes anxieties and fears manifest themselves as procrastination, depression, and perfectionism. Sometimes they don't go to the trouble of disguising themselves that way—they just nibble away at your stomach lining like piranhas. And in terms of your writing, they can be just as destructive as those ferocious little fishies.

I wonder sometimes whether I'd be a more successful writer today if it weren't for the anxiety disorders that dogged me for so many years. I'm happy to be at work on my second book and to have finally made a regular practice of both writing poetry and studying it in at least one annual class. But what if I'd been healthy and productive all that time in the past? Would I have completed that novel, that children's book? Would I be a well-established presence in the world of poetry? Would I be contributing important social commentary that makes the world a better place? Who knows?

The fact is, I found myself in a place where …

1. I had to accept that I wouldn't have children as I'd hoped, which made me think long and hard about what I wanted to do with my life.

2. I saw a young co-worker leave for lunch every day carrying his notebook, which made me think if he could do it, so could I.

3. I watched the World Trade Center collapse a mile from where I stood, which made me realize that if I wanted to write, I'd better do it now.

If you want to do it now, consider some of the following tips for combating anxiety and fear. I've benefited a lot from each of them, and I hope you'll find some of them effective, too.

Just Breathe

Breathing and progressive relaxation exercises can have a life-changing effect when they become habitual and internalized. This can happen after as little as a few weeks of practice. Simple instructions on these exercises are widely available, and I recommend that you do an online search, but here are a few basics you can use right away:

● Breathe through your nose, not your mouth.

● Breathe slowly, not quickly.

● Fill your whole torso with air, not just your chest.

● Sit and stand straight with your shoulders back instead of slumping.

● Unclench your fists.

● Unclench your jaw.

- Any time you notice that your shoulders are hunched up toward your ears, let them hang down—imagine your neck and shoulders in the shape of a coat hanger.

Turn to these practices the moment you feel anxiety building up, and you'll be surprised how much more calm and in control you can feel—and how much more clearly you can think.

Don't believe me? Read on: when I was younger, I had a terrible phobia about going to the dentist. It was so bad that I managed to avoid it completely for nearly 10 years. (Kids, don't try this at home—I'm still paying the price today!) When it could no longer be avoided (ow!), I went—but I'd spend days, even weeks, beforehand dreading it and fighting off the butterflies in my stomach.

But here's the funny part: eventually I started using relaxation exercises while at the dentist. And one day, I noticed that the moment I sat back in the chair, my entire body went limp like a pancake. I had trained myself so well that dentist appointments had become as relaxing as a massage. So take it from me: when it comes to relaxation exercises, miracles *can* happen.

Patience, Patience

John Berendt took the literary world by storm in 1994 with *Midnight in the Garden of Good and Evil*. It was nearly 11 years before he made his comeback with *The City of Falling Angels*.

Learn to Relax

The preceding breathing exercises might go a long way toward helping you relax, but you can further that along. For example, switch to decaf or herbal tea instead of coffee—or at least alternate between, or blend, caf and decaf.

Try a beginner-level yoga DVD or class once or twice a week. Go for the old-fashioned kind, not the strenuous power yoga. (*Hint:* if the DVD packaging emphasizes weight loss and the teacher looks really buff and shiny, it's probably the latter kind.) Other types of exercise are good for reducing anxiety, too, but yoga offers flexibility, balance, and strength for both the body *and* the mind.

Sleep. Few things can spike your anxiety and irritability level the way sleep deprivation can. And you might just dream up the next plot turn while you're catching up on your ZZZs.

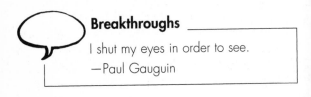

Breakthroughs

I shut my eyes in order to see.
—Paul Gauguin

Prayer and meditation don't just have spiritual benefits—they have physical benefits, too. If you don't think it's your kind of thing, give it a try anyway. A good writer is open-minded!

Go Gradually

A crucial exercise cognitive-behavioral therapists use in helping patients overcome phobias and anxieties is *gradual exposure*. For example, if someone is afraid of dogs, a therapist might have him start out by looking at pictures of dogs while breathing calmly, then have him walk past dogs on leashes or in fenced yards rather than crossing the street to avoid them, and then approaching and petting a dog.

You can apply the same principles to writing-related fears, like the fear of being criticized, making an error, or committing "accidental plagiarism." (I think we've all wrestled with that particular worry.) If this sounds like something that might help you, look into it—it's very often a short-term treatment and far more cost-effective than other types of therapy.

Ask for Feedback

If you're afraid of criticism, invite it in and surround yourself with it—this is the best way to learn that criticism doesn't have the power to destroy you (unless you let it). Plus, it can infuse you with a new awareness of your purpose in writing—communicating with readers—and drive you out of your lonely, overburdened head.

Best of all, if you can get reasonably honest and informed criticism—whether from a friend, writing classmate, or teacher—you'll gain valuable clues about what you're doing right and doing wrong.

One important caution, though: when choosing your reader, avoid anyone who routinely makes you feel bad about yourself or seems to be concerned more with making herself look smart and superior than with offering you constructive comments. You don't need a cheerleader, but you also don't need a ball and chain dragging you down.

Exercise: Buried Treasure

Going deep doesn't just help you clear out the bad stuff. It also helps you gain access to a lot of good stuff—stuff that can enrich your creativity tremendously. While you're rooting out perfectionism, procrastination, or whatever other tendencies that have been blocking you, try some of the following exercises to start getting under the surface and unearthing valuable material for your writing:

Clean out your wallet or pocketbook, examine the contents, and write about what comes to mind.

Think of two people who know you but who don't know each other. Imagine them meeting and discovering that you are a mutual friend and then getting into a conversation about you. Write down their conversation.

Think of a loss that upset you more than people realized. Write a page or two explaining to them what they didn't understand.

Imagine yourself in a situation that would provoke major anxiety for you but is extremely unlikely to cause you any real harm—for example, being stuck in an elevator, having a spider crawl up your leg, speaking in front of a roomful of strangers. Write about the experience, from beginning to end.

Describe yourself as a likable person. Then describe yourself as an unlikable person. (Both descriptions must be truthful.)

Breakthroughs

> Every child is an artist. The problem is how to remain an artist once he grows up.
> —Pablo Picasso

Analyze in an essay how you think your gender has affected your life. Do the same for your ethnic background, your economic background, your religious background, and your sexual orientation. Remember that the essay is about you, not others in or out of your group, and include personal anecdotes.

Write about what your favorite toy was during your childhood—and whether you think it says anything about who you are today.

Write about the hardest decision you ever had to make.

Write about something that might have happened years ago but still, to this day, makes you cry when you think about it. Keep writing even after you start crying.

Write about why you smoke cigarettes—or why you don't smoke cigarettes. Strive for honesty.

Write about why you believe in God—or why you don't believe in God. Strive for honesty.

In all the time you've been doing it, going back to the earliest years, what have been the three most rewarding or satisfying moments related to writing? Write about them.

Think through your typical weekday, and identify the three most joyous moments in it. Write about them.

Describe the clothes you feel the most comfortable in, and explain why.

Write your will.

Write your obituary. And then write the obituary you'd like to have.

Art is an adventure. As you experience it, you get to travel to all sorts of places, from deserts to oceans, from Outer Mongolia to outer space. And as both a reader and a writer, you also get to journey into some truly fascinating territory: the human heart and mind.

The Least You Need to Know

- Writer's block is often related to larger behavioral patterns, such as perfectionism and procrastination.
- Thinking calmly and logically goes a long way toward solving problems like writer's block.
- Criticism can't destroy you unless you allow it to.
- Facing your mistakes, your fears, and your difficult emotions makes you a better writer.

Things to Do Instead of Writing

In This Chapter

- What you need to do before—and after—writing
- Expand your horizons; expand your creativity
- Serving your writing career even when you're blocked
- Tips for making the submission process easier

In her book *The Midnight Disease: The Drive to Write, Writer's Block, and the Creative Brain,* Alice Flaherty discusses a condition called hypergraphia—essentially, compulsive writing. It's believed that none other than the great Russian novelist Fyodor Dostoevsky suffered from it, although as Flaherty is careful to point out, hypergraphia is no guarantee of *quality,* just *quantity.* The most common cause of hypergraphia, she says, is temporal lobe epilepsy. Dostoevsky also had to deal with uncontrollable thrashing limbs, terrible spells of fear and mental confusion, and a gambling problem, among other symptoms.

So hypergraphia is, in a way, the opposite of writer's block, and it makes writer's block look not so bad in comparison, doesn't it? But without all that compulsive writing, you sometimes find yourself with time on your hands.

Whether your block is temporary or chronic, it can be hard to find the right balance between writing and not writing. You might feel like you have to make an extra effort to write as much as possible to make up for the blocks, which creates a nagging sense of anxiety—which in turn only makes the block worse.

For any writer, blocked or not, it's important to make writing a priority, but at the same time, writing itself isn't the whole story. For one thing, if your goal is to be a good writer, you must do more than write—you must conceive your work before you write it. And if your goal is to be a published writer, you must do more than write—you must sell your work after your write it.

This chapter deals with both the "before" and the "after." First, we explore the idea that, to put a twist on Socrates' famous quotation, "The unlived life is not worth examining." Then I discuss some of the practical gruntwork you need to do to develop your writing career. During those times when you're having trouble sitting down and forming actual sentences, these are both good, productive alternatives to indulge in. You won't be, strictly speaking, *writing*—but you will be improving yourself as a writer and contributing to your future success.

The Unlived Life Is Not Worth Examining

You've no doubt heard the classic advice: write what you know. I agree with that advice, but I think there should be a Part 2: know more!

I often pick up a novel and read the cover only to discover that the protagonist is—once again—a writer. I'm a writer myself, so you'd think that would attract me, and to some extent it does. But after a while, it gets a little tired. I recently discovered a fiction writer named Anthony Doerr. His prose is gorgeous, and his plots are compelling … but that wasn't the main thing that made me an instant fan. What I loved was that his stories took place in remote Asian villages, in rural Montana, in Liberia. They featured characters who were very rich and characters who were very poor. I felt that sense of adventure, of journeying out into a big world, that reading gave me when I was a kid.

Block Crock

People like characters they can identify with. Yes—but it's not only about identifying with characters' jobs or ethnic backgrounds or marital status. It's about identifying with them as fellow humans who experience universal emotions. And it's all the more rewarding for readers when characters who seem foreign at first turn out to be people just like them.

So many contemporary novels seem to be stuck in the same little worlds. There's nothing inherently wrong with these settings. Alison Lurie and David Lodge write terrific books set in the world of academia, but when every third novel out there seems to star a professor of literature, readers can start longing for a change.

I've got an awful lot of poems about being a poet lying around, so I know how easy it is to fall into the trap of writing what you know. And of course, some worlds are inherently dramatic and will always be fiction staples, like law enforcement and medicine. But as a reader, I also know how wonderful it is to feel that an author is showing me things I'd never get to see without his or her help. I've read lots of mysteries, but my favorites are the Arkady Renko novels by Martin Cruz Smith, which have taken me to Soviet Russia, Cuba, and Chernobyl. Smith uses a police detective—not an unusual character in the book world—but makes him additionally intriguing by putting him in settings and steeping him in a culture thoroughly unfamiliar to Americans.

Block Crock

Write what you know. Sure, but the more you know, the more you can write about. Remember that the word *novel* also means "new." Keep learning new things to bring to your readers.

You don't have to be a daredevil or a world traveler along the lines of Ernest Hemingway to expand your repertoire. You can do many things—some quite easy and ordinary—to add depth and breadth to your writing. Consider some of the following.

Interact with Different People

Many writers are shy people. I know I've always found writing easier than talking. But if your work and social life keep you in an insular and homogenous community where everyone comes from the same socioeconomic background or ethnicity and shares the same interests, you might be missing out.

Dump any lingering high-school mind-set that categorizes people as jocks or nerds or yuppies or slackers or whatever, and listen and learn from everyone. Instead of making meaningless small talk about the weather with an architect or plumber or hairdresser, try asking them some questions about their job—how they got into it, what they like about it, and what they don't. (Don't set up a tape recorder, though; that could be a little off-putting.)

You might discover great story ideas by chatting with anyone from your kids' soccer coach, to the flight attendant on your plane, to the guy who sells you your coffee every morning. You'll also be less likely to create unrealistic or stereotypical characters.

Learn Something

Ask Grandma for a sewing lesson. Have your auto-mechanic friend demonstrate his skills for you.

Watch your computer programmer cousin do her thing. Take an evening class in carpentry or cooking. Sign up for piano lessons. Knowledge of these kinds of things will help you add detail and texture to your fiction. And you might even pick up some lucrative skills to help pay the bills while you're waiting for that big advance!

Travel—Far or Near

If you can't afford to be an international globetrotter, keep in mind that new worlds are sometimes only a few miles, or even a few blocks, away. Cheap bus fares and budget motels can make lots of little adventures possible. Splitting the driving and the gas with a few friends might enable you to see new cities. And if you live in a city, you can do a lot of exploring with nothing but train fare—or even your own two feet. Tourist destinations are oriented toward leisure and scenery, but travel is different from tourism—and it tends to be cheaper and more interesting.

Read Adventurously

Stephen Crane famously portrayed the experiences of a Civil War soldier in *The Red Badge of Courage* without ever setting foot on a battlefield. So don't think "write what you know" restricts you unduly. Reading others' accounts—in newspapers, magazines, and books—and watching documentary footage can provide you with enough basic knowledge of a place or situation to make your fictional settings and characters detailed and believable.

> **Breakthroughs**
>
> To acquire the habit of reading is to construct for yourself a refuge from almost all the miseries of life.
>
> —W. Somerset Maugham

Observe Closely

Having lots of new experiences is good for your writing, but if you race through them without paying enough attention, as if you're trying to complete your Checklist of Adventures, you won't get the full benefit. You want depth, not just breadth. So in addition to seeking out new things, you can also turn everyday, routine activities into opportunities for learning if you observe more closely than usual.

How does the train you take every day work? How exactly is the guy behind the counter making that pizza? How is that spider building its web? Watch babies. Watch animals. See the world—up close.

Take a Daydream Break

When you fill every moment with activity and get into a goal-oriented mind-set, your imagination atrophies. Creativity sometimes seems like the proverbial "butterfly of happiness" that's impossible to catch but will come alight on your shoulder if you sit still long enough.

If you're a writer—especially a fiction writer—odds are you were a big daydreamer as a child. Your parents and teachers might have even complained about it. But while it might not have served you well during math class, it turns out daydreaming is a powerful tool for a writer. When you let your imagination play freely, it can lead you not only to plots and themes for your writing, but to a greater degree of self-knowledge and emotional understanding. So build some time into your busy day for a little daydreaming!

Breakthroughs

To do great work a man must be very idle as well as very industrious.

—Samuel Butler

Develop Style *and* Substance

A good writer has an open mind—not an empty one. Without an underlying philosophy, a set of values, or a point of view, writing can turn to mush, no matter how pretty it may be on the surface.

Take stock every once in a while, and think about the ideas and beliefs you're committed to. Are your actions, and your writing, consistent? Are you comfortable with them deep down? Do you need to adjust any ideas or beliefs based on new information you've learned? What do you think is the right way to act? What do you consider truly important?

Sometimes persistent writer's block can be rooted in the lack of a sense of self—a confusion about what we really think, feel, and believe that keeps us from forming an essential core around which our writing can be built.

Be Good at Something Else

If writing is the only thing that makes you feel competent or worthwhile, writer's block is going to be pretty devastating. Make yourself a little list of other things you can do well—no matter how irrelevant they might seem:

I'm good at …

- organizing closets.
- roller-skating.
- frosting cakes.
- reading maps.

Then think of something you'd like to be better at—dancing, cooking, using a particular computer program—and spend some time improving that skill. Competence of any kind is a good feeling, and the knowledge that you're capable of excelling at other things is a big psychological boost during periods of frustrating writer's block.

Breakthroughs

To escape criticism—do nothing, say nothing, be nothing.

—Elbert Hubbard

Get Perspective

Living in a nation whose size and culture make it so dominant, we sometimes forget that people think and live in vastly different ways in other corners of the globe. It helps sometimes to take a step back and get some perspective. Watch the news. Seek out the international news page, or look for actual foreign news sources on cable TV and the Internet.

Similarly, keep in mind that our moment in history is one point on a very long timeline, and that understanding the events of 50 or 500 years ago can go a long way toward understanding why our world is the way it is today. If you habitually avoid "historical stuff" because it seems irrelevant or dull, give it another try via popular history books or historically set novels. (For the best selections, look for reviews that praise the author's research and accuracy.) You might find yourself fascinated as you discover parallels between the old and the new—and you'll also be a more informed and imaginative writer.

Eat, Drink, and Be Merry

Writing is work. You might enjoy it, but it's still work. You might consider it a noble pursuit for the good of humankind, but it's still work. You might not get paid for it, but it's still work.

Be sure you also have play and pleasure and relaxation in your life along with all that work. And being a teetotaler on a diet is not an excuse—just eat roasted peppers, drink peppermint tea, and do whatever else it is that makes you merry.

Breakthroughs

Books are good enough in their way, but they are a mighty blood-less substitute for life.

—Robert Louis Stevenson

Attack That Gruntwork

Unless you're wealthy enough to maintain a staff of servants, every job, including the artist's job, comes with some gruntwork. And it's a good thing, too, because no one is in peak form every moment of the day, and semi-mindless but necessary tasks are a good way to get something done when you're not up to the more challenging demands of your chosen field.

As a writer who, presumably, wants to get published (or continue getting published), you have to attend to the business end of your field, not just the creative end. In the following sections, I share some tips for making productive use of your downtime and brief periods of writer's block. Of course, you can't submit manuscripts if you haven't written anything, but if you need to rest up and untangle your brain a bit, these activities will keep you busy—and might even inspire you to get back to the creative work.

Expand Your Product Line and Markets

One of my poetry teachers advised me to send out lots of stuff. Up until then, I had chosen only what I thought was my very best work and sent it to a small selection of publications I thought might be receptive. I followed his advice and started sending out more poems, more frequently. And I did get results—I immediately started getting more rejection letters, more frequently.

But there's no arguing that you have to cast a wide net if you're trying to get published. You don't want to mass-mail your manuscripts as if they were spam, but you also can't try too hard to determine what's worth sending out and who might or might not like it. If you've got a list of pieces you send out routinely, look over some of your other work and see if you can expand the list. (That short story might be better than you think!) And even if you're not 100 percent sure that magazine or small press likes your particular style, it could be worth a try. The editor there who happens to read your submission might just be the one who loves it and pushes for it with her boss.

Use the Internet to get a sense of what different publications and publishers are looking for. And when poring over *Writer's Market* or other such resources, don't skip—skim. The title of the publication alone might be misleading, and if you skip to the next one, you might be missing a potential buyer for your work. If you write sonnets, you can probably skip the entry for *Horror Tales Monthly*, but many more eclectic journals have names that don't immediately convey what sort of submissions they're open to.

Stuff and Stamp

Having a frustrating afternoon in front of the keyboard on a rainy day? It might be time to lug out a pile of manila envelopes, a roll of stamps, and a pen, and prepare a pile for the post office.

Block Crock

Sending stuff out is such a hassle. I'm not going to bother unless it seems really worthwhile.   It's a hassle, but a necessary hassle. Some places allow e-mail submissions nowadays, but until that's standard policy, you're going to have to knuckle down and do some paperwork if you want to maximize your chances of getting published.

Putting together submissions can be surprisingly time-consuming and nerve-racking, what with SASEs (self-addressed stamped envelopes) and cover letters and one magazine ordering you to staple and another proclaiming "No staples … ever!" I recommend a methodical approach to avoid errors and wasted time. You'll most likely figure out a system that works for you after a little trial and error, but if it helps, here's my own step-by-step process:

In a small spiral notebook, I write down the mailing address, editor's name, and requirements of promising publications I come across in my research.

"Requirements" means anything I need to know when preparing a submission, such as the following:

- SASE required
- No submissions between June 1 and September 1
- Maximum of five poems per submission
- No poems more than 60 lines long
- Submissions must be double-spaced

I leave plenty of room after each entry, because more information will be added later, including the eventual response.

Then, when I have a few places accumulated on the list and I'm ready to send out a new batch, I look at my pile of poems and consider which ones to send to which publications. (I try to stick to places that allow multiple submissions, but keeping track helps me avoid submitting a poem elsewhere when it's already with an "exclusive" journal for consideration. It also helps me avoid the embarrassment of sending the same poem to the same journal twice!) I jot down the titles of the poems next to each mailing address.

When I know what I'm sending out, what the requirements are, and how many copies of each poem I need, I can see what I have to do. Competition entries should, in most cases, have no identifying information on them, while regular submissions should include your name, address, phone, and e-mail. I might have only two hard copies of a particular poem, but I'm planning to send it to three different publications. So I hit the computer and do whatever editing and printing needs to be done.

> **Breakthroughs**
>
> We must carry the arts to the people, not wait for the people to come to the arts.
> —Arthur Mitchell

Still at the computer, with my little submission notebook at my side, I work on the necessary cover letters. Thank heavens for word processing, because I can use one letter as a template and adjust the headings and tweak the content on a case-by-case basis. Of course, I do this *very* carefully and always proofread before sending.

Time to make the doughnuts ... I mean, the piles. For each submission, I stack up the following:

- Addressed envelope
- Cover letter
- Manuscript
- SASE
- Stamp(s)
- In the case of competitions with fees, the check

(*Bonus timesaver tip:* in advance, perhaps while watching television, address a bunch of SASEs and manila envelopes, so they're ready and waiting for you.) I stuff ... I stamp ... and I send. Ahhh ... what an accomplishment. What a feeling of hope. Now I have to get back to some actual writing ....

Copyedit and Proofread

As a former book editor, I can tell you that the editing process is longer and more complicated than you might imagine. If you're not a published author yet, you might not realize that most books go through numerous reads and countless changes before they actually hit the store shelves.

An *acquisitions editor* might ask for a general revision, recommending significant changes to the plot or characters or the way the content is organized. A *line editor*—sometimes the same person, sometimes not—will read the book carefully and make or suggest smaller changes, focusing more on style and sentence structure. Then a *copy editor* will comb through it, fixing errors of fact, logical consistency, grammar, spelling, and more. A *proofreader* will look at a printout of the book and fix typos or errors the previous editors might have missed. Depending on the project and the publisher, the typeset pages might be sent back for you, the author, to read over at this point. And some books get a "slug," in which someone makes a final check to ensure that corrections have been made and that page numbers and other details are all in order.

If your writer's block is related to a problem with perfectionism, that information should be a source of comfort! But it also means that by doing some of that work now, you can make the process a lot easier for yourself (and your publisher) later.

And when it comes to getting your work accepted, keep in mind that while spelling errors probably won't hurt your chances if the book overall is interesting and well written, any error can prove distracting to a busy editor, and you don't want her reading experience to be colored by too many mistakes in the text. Set aside blocked periods of time to look at some of your completed work, reading it carefully for the kinds of errors copy editors and proofreaders look for. Fix typos and spelling and punctuation mistakes. If an editor is going to buy one historical romance this month, and there are two on her desk that are both good, she just might lean toward the one that *isn't* riddled with messy mistakes.

Block Crock

They have people to fix my spelling.
They do have people to fix your spelling after the book has been bought—but if an overworked acquisitions editor can barely follow your plot because of all the misspellings and bad punctuation, she might just take a pass instead of continuing to read.

Make an Idea List

Ideas, big and little, flit through our minds all the time. Even if you're keeping your notebook(s) nearby, as suggested earlier, it can be helpful to make a one-page "Possible Future Projects" list you can hang up near your computer and jot down raw ideas like "novel about environmental disaster" or "essay comparing pre- and post-Internet culture."

When you're stuck in the middle of your current project, your idea list will remind you that this block is only temporary. And even if you do decide your latest piece just isn't working out and you wind up trashing it, you've got plenty of other ideas waiting.

Do Your Homework

Whether you're writing fiction or nonfiction, research is almost always part of the job. When you're feeling unproductive, get online or hit the library and find the facts that will fill in the blanks in your work.

And speaking of filling in the blanks, I highly recommend using "tk"—journalistic shorthand for "to come"—while writing. If you know there's a name or number or detail you need to look up, don't interrupt your flow; just put "tk" and keep going. You can look it up later, and the "tk" will serve as a reminder when you read it over that something's missing. You can even use "tk" when you're having trouble finding the just-right word in the moment, and mull it over after you're done instead. One cautionary note: skim through for any remaining "tk"s before you send your piece to an editor.

Promote Yourself

You don't have to be on a book tour—or even be a published writer—to engage in a little self-promotion. Simply sending out some work to friends or colleagues is a form of self-promotion. If you're a freelancer or in the beginning stages of building a writing career, setting up lunch dates with professional contacts or just dropping e-mails to say "hi," will help keep you in the forefront of their minds, and might result in additional assignments.

If you're a fairly established writer with a website, take a little time to update or expand it, and send out an e-mail with a link to your "writing mailing list" letting them know that it's been updated.

You might also want to take a page from the big-corporation playbook and add your website address to outgoing correspondence, submission letters, and anything else that goes to people who might help you find work.

Run Errands

The post office, the copy shop, the stationery store, the library—if you're getting stir-crazy in your writing chair, getting out, getting something done, and seeing the world can be a big help.

Plus, you never know when or where you'll meet new, interesting people or get an idea for your next piece. Keep your eyes open!

Clean Up

A dirty or disorganized environment probably isn't helping your concentration, so if you're blocked, a little scrubbing and stacking could give you a way to pass the time, *and* a better chance at success when you return to your task.

However, if your house could serve as a film set for a Swiffer commercial, you're probably just procrastinating and should get back to work.

In the world of film, there's a time when the cameras are rolling, but a lot of what makes the movie work takes place in pre- and post-production. The same goes for your writing, so take advantage of downtime to dedicate yourself to your art in other ways.

The Least You Need to Know

- Nonwriting time is not wasted time—unless you waste it.
- You don't have to climb mountains to be adventurous.
- Point of view is a big part of writing, so figure out what yours is.
- Editing, preparing submissions, doing research, and daydreaming are among the many profitable ways you can spend time during blocks.

Body Block

In This Chapter

- The physical side of writing
- Preventing ailments that can interfere with writing
- Protecting your hands and back while at the keyboard
- Tips on proper posture

We tend to separate different kinds of work into categories: some work is labeled as *manual* or *physical labor*; other work is called *cerebral* or *intellectual*. But no job is purely one or the other. As sedentary as a writer's life might seem, plenty of physical factors can affect his or her performance. After all, the brain is a bodily organ, too!

In this chapter, I briefly review some of the ways your body might be blocking you—and some things you can do to ensure that you're functioning in peak physical form.

Body Check

Take a head-to-toe review and see whether a physical problem could be interfering with your work. Not every problem is easy to identify, so pay close attention to any aches or physical difficulties you may be experiencing. Sometimes a recurring strain takes a while to start hurting. Sometimes you don't even hurt so much as feel a nagging discomfort that's hard to trace to its original source. When you get your body tuned up, you'll probably find that your mind works better, too.

Get Your Eyes Checked

If you find it hard to concentrate while writing (or reading), that might be a sign of a vision problem—especially if you've passed your thirty-fifth birthday. If your eye doctor says you're okay and you don't need corrective lenses, you can try easing the strain on your eyes by setting the window on your monitor to 110 percent or 125 percent rather than 100 percent. It doesn't change the font size of the actual type, but it makes it look bigger (and makes it easier to read) on-screen.

Also, take periodic breaks from staring at your monitor, and consider using a water-mister for dry eyes. If you're a voracious reader—as most writers are—you might even want to browse through the large-print section next time you're at the library. The type in regular books can often be very small and crowded, and large print can provide a more relaxed reading experience.

Put the Brakes on Headaches

Headaches, of course, have numerous and complex causes, and if you have severe, persistent, or recurring headaches, you should be checked out by a doctor. Many times, you can prevent common tension headaches—which can afflict writers who spend hours in front of their keyboards—with a few simple steps:

Stay well hydrated throughout the day, and keep a water bottle on your writing desk. Don't wait until you actually feel thirsty to drink.

Keep alcohol, tobacco, and junk food intake to a minimum, if you must have it at all.

Don't overdo the caffeine. One or two cups might perk you up and help you focus on your writing, but repeated refills can get your brain hooked and lead to withdrawal headaches—and ultimately make it harder to concentrate on your work when you get so jittery you can't think straight.

Take a stretch break every 20 minutes or so. Muscles tend to tighten up when you're hunched in front of a computer or over a notebook, and that can lead directly to headaches. (Even better, don't hunch in the first place. See the following "Posture Pointers" section.)

Get enough sleep, and take naps if you need to, but keep them to 15 minutes long. Any longer than that, and you risk falling into a deeper level of sleep, which can leave you groggy and headachy when you try to get up.

A Cramp in Your Style

You've probably heard of *writer's cramp*. But you might not know that it's actually a chronic neurological condition in which sufferers experience uncontrollable hand and arm movements and have great difficulty holding a pen, and it's pretty rare.

Footnotes

Henry James was a victim of writer's cramp, and in the later years of his career, he had to switch from using a pen to dictating.

Much more common is *carpal tunnel syndrome*, which is caused when a nerve is pinched from overuse. Carpal tunnel syndrome can happen to people who spend a lot of time at computers or make frequent repetitive motions, such as craft workers or musicians do. On its website, the Mayo Clinic points out that there's no proven way to prevent carpal tunnel syndrome, but it does offer some suggestions for protecting your hands from potential ailments:

- Use a big pen with an oversized, soft grip adapter, so you won't need to grip the pen too tightly.

- Reduce your force—don't pound away at the keyboard.

- Give your hands and wrists frequent breaks by gently stretching them every 15 to 20 minutes.

- Keep your keyboard at elbow height or slightly lower.

- Improve your posture so your shoulders don't roll forward.

- Keep your hands warm—if you can't raise the thermostat where you're working, try fingerless gloves.

Block Crock

I'm an artist, not a jock.   Despite the popular image of arty types as pale, malnourished, and drunk, taking care of yourself is a much better way to lengthen your writing career. You don't need to be a gym rat; you do need to forget about stereotypes and balance your intellectual pursuits with a healthy respect for your body's needs.

Get Your Back Up

If you're lucky, you'll be barely aware you *have* a back for many years to come. But with age—and lots of time at your writing desk—you'll likely be reminded of its existence, and not necessarily in a pleasant way. Put that day off for as long as possible by getting up every once in a while, placing your hands on your lower back, and leaning back gently. If your chair doesn't offer enough support, pamper your lower back by putting a small pillow behind it.

And don't let the writer's life lead to excess weight—it doesn't take too much poundage to put additional strain on your back (not to mention your heart and other important parts of you). Taking care of your back now can save you a lot of lost work time later.

Posture Pointers

All that nagging to "sit up straight" during your childhood was good advice. When your posture is not ideal, you don't usually feel the effects at first—in fact, you might even think you feel more comfortable in a slumpy slouch. But your body is designed to support itself best in certain positions, and over time, putting too much of your weight in the wrong places can cause all sorts of problems.

The government's Occupational Safety and Health Administration (OSHA), which seeks to prevent injuries in the workplace, offers some guidelines for people working at computers, including the following:

- When typing, your hands, wrists, and forearms should form a straight line and be roughly parallel to the floor.

- Your elbows should be close to your body and bent at an angle between 90 and 120 degrees. (If your memories of high school geometry have faded, a 90-degree angle is a right angle—that is, an L shape. A 120-degree angle would be about the angle of the hands on a clock when it's 4 o'clock.)

- Your feet should be flat on the floor or on a footrest.

- Your back should be fully supported when you sit vertically or lean back slightly.

- Your thighs and hips should be roughly parallel to the floor and supported by a well-padded seat. (The well-padded seat of a chair, that is.)

- Your knees should be at about the same height as your hips, and your feet on the floor should be placed just slightly forward of your knees.

- The top of your computer monitor should be at, or slightly below, your eye level.

- Your head should be pretty much in line with your torso, either level or bent slightly forward.

In addition to these guidelines, you can also try signing up for some yoga classes.

Block Crock

I have to hunch over to see the screen! Get your eyes checked, adjust your font size, get a bigger monitor, but don't hunch, or you might wind up having trouble even sitting in front of the screen.

Good posture can feel a little strange at first when you're not used to it. If you've been slumping, you've been training your muscles to go in certain directions—even if they're not necessarily the best directions for them to go. When you've adjusted, though, you're likely to find yourself feeling stronger and more relaxed. Plus, you'll likely experience a lot fewer aches and pains in the future—and get more writing done.

The Least You Need to Know

- All work is physical—including writing.
- Discomfort can drive you away from your work, so care for your body as well as your mind.
- Prevent back problems by keeping at your "writing weight" and maintaining good posture at the keyboard.
- Take frequent breaks to stretch—and remember to sit up straight!

From Beginning to End

In This Chapter

- Writing means being your own boss
- Yes, beginnings and endings are scary
- Seven ideas to help you get started
- Six ideas to help you finish

Writer's block often takes one of two distinct forms: problems getting started or problems getting finished. As mentioned in Chapter 6, writing is highly subjective and unpredictable. It's hard to apply tools like checklists and measurements to creative pursuits. So just as you can't grade a novel (or poem, essay, etc.) the way you grade a spelling test, you also can't easily pinpoint where that novel should begin and end. It's really up to you to make the call. Lots of help-wanted ads emphasize that they're looking for "self-starters" who can "work independently"—and if there were help-wanted ads for creative writers, those would certainly be among the top requirements.

As an artist, you're left with utter freedom ... and freedom can be scary sometimes. With so many creative possibilities, so many word choices, and so many directions you can go, it's no wonder some of us get overwhelmed or even mentally paralyzed looking at the blank page. Similarly, when no one is expecting your story by 5 P.M. on Friday, it's very easy to keep reworking it or take longer and longer breaks, refusing to make the decisions needed to complete the work. But when you don't have an annoying boss setting the agenda, breathing down your neck, and yelling about deadlines, you pretty much have to be the annoying boss yourself if you want to get anything done.

This chapter addresses both of these obstacles. Whether you're struggling to get your engine to turn over or stalling repeatedly on your way to your destination—or both—the ideas in this chapter should make for a smoother ride.

Getting Started

Do you spend a lot of time staring at a blank page (or a blank screen)? Or do you seem to be able to find every excuse not to get near a blank page or screen in the first place? Both getting started and getting finished require a commitment—and sometimes, a hard push. Let's take a look at some of the things that might interfere with getting into the writing groove, as well as some ways to overcome them.

Footnotes

French writer Molière commented: "I always do the first line well, but I have trouble doing the others."

Cold Feet

Many a groom- or bride-to-be has struggled with the commitment they're about to make. And it's not necessarily because they don't truly love their betrothed. It's just that they can't help wondering, *Is there someone better out there for me? Am I really ready to give up all those other possibilities?*

The good news is that once you start—and finish— your story or poem, you can fall in love with the next one, no guilt required. In fact, unlike with a spouse, you can even change your story or poem to meet your own specifications.

When you're starting a new piece, you might fear, even subconsciously, that you're making a big mistake. What if you invest a lot of time in this idea and it turns out to be a dud? Keep in mind that even if this idea doesn't pan out, you can't know for sure until you give it a shot. If the idea piques your interest enough to get you thinking about writing, there is *something* to it, and you need to explore it and see where it takes you. If you invest a paragraph, a page, or even a couple chapters, you'll have a much clearer sense of whether it's worth it to keep going. You can't decide that before you even start working on it. Save your mulling for more serious and lasting commitments. The blank page is more like a first date—you can keep things casual and see where it goes.

Waiting for "Inspiration"

As mentioned in previous chapters, sometimes we writers tend to be a little too mystical about what we do. If you tend to think, on more than an occasional basis, things like *I'll know when the time is right*, or *I haven't quite hit on* the *idea yet*, or *I just don't feel inspired*, the root of your block could be a type of passivity. You're relying on some sort of outside force to come along and sweep you away, making the right creative decision clear for you without you having to think too hard about it. In reality, you should approach writing as "1 percent inspiration and 99 percent perspiration."

Another seductive aspect of the "waiting for inspiration" habit is that when inspiration does happen, it feels so good. Those magical moments when a great idea takes shape seemingly out of the blue, and the words flow effortlessly, are wonderful. But to return to our previous analogy, relying too much on inspiration would be like expecting a relationship to consist of nothing but romantic peaks, without any of the valleys in between. To put it bluntly, it ain't gonna happen. Enjoy the peaks when they do come along, but don't give up the minute things get a little more challenging.

The Power of Ritual

When it's time to get into the Christmas spirit, we decorate the tree. When we need to get psyched for the big game, we listen to a pep talk from the coach. When Spinal Tap is about to go onstage, they yell "Rock and roll!"

Rituals serve not only to put us into a certain frame of mind, but also to mark beginnings, endings, and important milestones. You might want to establish a little ritual to help you get in the mood and distinguish a certain period of time as dedicated to writing. One talented writer I know suggests lighting a candle and saying an affirmation—perhaps something like "I'm going to create something good today," or "Right now, I'm doing what I love."

Breakthroughs

Nothing so difficult as a beginning
In poesy, unless perhaps the end.

—Lord Byron

(*Poesy* is an old term for the art of poetry. Yes, I had to look it up ....)

Your ritual doesn't need to be anything particularly reverent or spiritual. You might prefer to brew some mango tea, or place a vase of flowers next to your computer, or kiss your troll doll. Just find something that works for you and says "this next hour (or two or three) is my writing time."

Something to Work With

At my day job, I sometimes write, and I sometimes edit others' writing. I can tell you for sure that the latter task is easier—even when the editing required is extensive enough to border on rewriting— because instead of a blank page, there's something to work with, something to grab on to.

When you're trying to get started on that blank page, keep in mind that once you fill it up, no matter how lousy it may or may not be, you'll have made your job a lot easier. Now you'll have something to work with!

Start Somewhere Else

When something in the world gets caught like a fishhook in your mind or heart, it's probably a creative opportunity—even if you're not quite sure at first why it snagged you. These can be starting points for writing, but the tricky part is that they don't always belong at the beginning. Inspiration doesn't come in an orderly way—it's up to you as the artist to sort it into a comprehensible structure.

Sometimes the image that arrested your attention or the event that stirred your emotions winds up in the middle or at the end of the piece—but you need to start with it and work from there, whether you wind up going sideways, backward, or round and round. Try writing your "starting point" in the middle or the end of the page instead of the beginning, and see what happens.

Start Three Times

If you have a topic or theme in mind but can't get the actual writing going, try this: start the piece three times, three different ways. For example, you feel a poem brewing after walking through a rainstorm, but you just don't know how to begin. You know there was something about that experience that made you want to write about it, but what? What is it you really want to convey?

On three different pages, write three different possible openings. Maybe one starts out with the feeling of water seeping into your socks as you trudge down the street. Another focuses on the fear inspired by the loud cracks of lightning. The third reminisces about a storm you traveled through as a child. When you have three different openings in front of you, one will likely call to you more than the others, and you'll know which direction to go.

And if you still can't decide, you can write three poems instead of one!

Dive Right In

Okay, that's all well and good if you have an idea in the first place. What if your mind is as blank as the page in front of you?

Aimless writing can be a good exercise in itself—and it can often lead you to ideas you didn't even know you had. My own output increased a lot when I started making a point of taking my notebook to lunch with me. If I just sat there with the notebook open in front of me for a half hour while I ate my sandwich and watched the world go by—and never wrote a single thing—that was fine. But more often than not, some little scene or event would catch my attention, or my mind would wander somewhere unexpected, and I would write something after all.

Block Crock

How can I get started if I don't have the slightest idea how to start? Sometimes the starting point doesn't reveal itself until you've already written half the piece. In fact, experienced writers often find that they go back and delete what seemed like the beginning point but was actually just a bout of clearing their throat and gathering their thoughts before they reached the *real* opening.

Perhaps 50 percent or more of that writing wound up going nowhere—a few scribbled lines or phrases, an exploration, a dead end. Sometimes I'd even complete a poem that, when I reread it later, made me say "Yech." But a lot of good work came out of it, too, and if I didn't regularly "dive in" without a map or a clue, a lot of my work wouldn't exist.

Try the dive-in approach for two weeks, whether it's while you're on your lunch hour, taking the train home, or drinking your morning coffee. Or take your notebook to some of the places suggested in Chapter 2. There's nothing to lose, and a lot to gain.

Getting Finished

Do you have a lot of half-baked bits and pieces of writing lying around? Do you run out of steam a lot and find yourself saying, "One of these days I have to get back to that"?

There's nothing wrong with giving up on an idea that isn't working, but if this is a long-term pattern, it might be *you* who isn't working. Not because you're goofing off—after all, you probably plunge into one project after another ... it's just that you don't seem to finish them.

> **Breakthroughs**
>
> There is always a point in every novel you're writing when you either want to flush it or burn it. This is inevitable. The trick is not to do any of those things.
>
> —Octavia Butler

Like getting started, getting finished can push your commitment buttons. Beginnings and endings of any kind—not just in writing—tend to feel a little momentous and can churn up a bit of stress. When you're coming close to completion in your writing, you know in the back of your mind that once you're done, the next step is to share your work with the world—and if that makes you nervous enough, maybe you'll do anything to avoid it, including repeatedly hitting the Start Over button.

And it's not difficult to keep finding excuses, because once again, writing is scarily subjective. Maybe you reread your work from 12 different angles, finding something that supposedly needs fixing every time. If you keep reworking and rethinking long enough, you'll get bored and then voilà—you toss it aside because … *it's boring*.

> ### Breakthroughs
>
> Passion is the quickest to develop, and the quickest to fade. Intimacy develops more slowly, and commitment more gradually still.
> —Robert J. Sternberg

The following ideas can help push you through to The End … so you can get to the next beginning.

End with a Period

If you've been stuck on a piece of writing too long, end it. Just end it. Print it out. Put it in an envelope. Send it out.

Wait a second … as you reach for the mailbox handle, is the next stanza or chapter suddenly coming to you in a rush? Now bring it back home and finish it for real.

Take a Tip from Hollywood

Nowadays, films on DVDs are released with multiple alternate endings. I don't need to see three different conclusions to the same movie as if I was trapped in some sort of futuristic physics experiment. But as a creative method, trying several endings can lead you to the right ending.

Go back to the point where you got stuck and diverge in a few directions, and you can get a feel for which one is successfully taking you to the next step and follow it from there. (Just don't bring in a focus group.)

Write Backward

Mystery writers do it, and you can, too. Ask yourself where you want to end up—even if you haven't yet figured out how to get there. When you can imagine and sketch out the ending—independent of the rest of the piece—getting there will be a lot easier.

Find What's Worth Finishing

Look at the things you've left in limbo, and determine which ones have died a natural death and which can and should be revived. If rereading it is enjoyable—and especially if rereading sparks new ideas—chances are there's life left in it yet.

You can also try tossing unfinished projects into a wastebasket. If it makes you feel truly sad to part with a particular one, pull it back out.

And if you have an honest writing buddy, ask her to look at a few of your partial manuscripts and tell you which ones she wants to see more of.

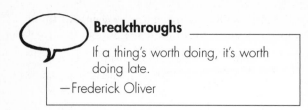

Breakthroughs

If a thing's worth doing, it's worth doing late.

—Frederick Oliver

Finish, Start, Finish

Now that you've created your "to be finished" pile, make a rule: before you start the next new project, you have to complete one that's been gathering dust. Alternate between starts and finishes until those promising-but-incomplete stories or poems are all done.

Reassess

Sometimes, when you start a long-term project like a novel or a memoir, you have a certain idea of what it's going to turn out like. That idea might be hazy, but you think you know what you're doing. And then the wild, wonderful process of creativity takes over, and the book might turn into something you didn't quite expect.

If you've hit the wall with a major writing project, you might need to take a step back and ask a few questions:

- How did I envision this project when I started?

- Has it taken me places I wasn't planning to go?

- Does it scare me a little now when I think about it? If so, why?
- What do I think about this project now?
- Am I willing to follow it where it leads?

If the book has really dragged on, say for a few years or more, you might also find that you have changed over time—and that you don't quite relate to the book the way you used to. You may feel that it no longer accurately represents your voice. It could be that your point of view of something has shifted, and as a result, the point of view in your book needs to shift, too. It's up to you to answer those questions, and once you do, the obstacles to finishing can become a lot easier to leap over.

The Least You Need to Know

- Blocks often happen at the beginning and the end of a project.
- Writers need to be "self-starters."
- Starting and finishing mean making commitments—but generally, they're not irreversible, lifelong commitments.
- Writing can take us places we didn't expect, and if you're feeling lost or nervous, it helps to take a step back and look at the big picture.

Clicks and Sparks

In This Chapter

- More complex and challenging exercises
- Assorted words and phrases to get you free-styling

I hope the information and material in the preceding chapters has helped you eliminate some of the obstacles that keep you from writing—and has re-invigorated you for new creative efforts. To help you get a fresh start, this chapter offers both exercises and prompts you can use as jumping-off points. Enjoy!

Advanced Exercises

These exercises might be a bit more complex and challenging than the exercises in previous chapters, but they serve the same basic purpose: to get you in the groove. Try some or all of them, and see if you're feeling more confident and capable as a writer. My guess is you are—and if you keep up your writing practice, no matter what, you'll just keep getting better.

A 12-year-old has just overheard her mother telling someone on the phone that she's pregnant. Continue the story.

A resident of what will one day be known as Manhattan is watching a ship full of Europeans approach the river's edge. Continue the story.

Write a two-page poem about one of the biggest disappointments you have experienced in life.

The dictator of a small country has just discovered he has cancer. Continue the story.

Write your speech announcing your candidacy for president of the United States.

Two slaves are trying to convince a fellow slave to join in a dangerous escape attempt. Continue the story.

Write a poem from the point of view of a horse.

Re-create the Romeo and Juliet story with a modern-day twist.

Compare and contrast your favorite movie with your favorite novel.

Describe the last trip you took—even if it was to the grocery store—as if you were writing a travel essay about an exotic destination.

Breakthroughs

Art flourishes where there is a sense of adventure.
—Alfred North Whitehead

An 80-year-old man on his deathbed has a story to tell. Tell it.

Write a story that seems to be about victory but is really about loss.

Write a story that seems to be about loss but is really about victory.

Write a story that involves a closet, a rose garden, and a broken dish.

Write a story about a family in a rural, isolated area seeing television for the first time.

Write a scene from the middle of a play featuring an angry character, a religiously devout character, and a narcissistic character.

Write a story that takes place 30 years from today.

Write an essay about how a political issue in the news has affected you as an individual.

Write a story in which the main character is in the middle of a crowd when he finds out he just won the lottery.

Write a poem that compares a human being to a plant.

Write the opening chapter of your biography, in the third person.

Starting Points

The following are prompts—that is, words, phrases, and sentences to help lead you into pure creativity.

Some have multiple meanings that will bring completely different associations to your mind than they would to someone else. Some are ordinary; others are on the odd side.

The direction in which you take them is entirely up to you. You can free-associate or meditate; you can try using a noun as a verb or vice versa. A prompt might serve as the opening line of a novel, a bit of dialogue, or a topic for a poem. And you might wind up forgetting the original prompt altogether as you take detour after detour onto brand-new creative roads. It's up to you, so start writing:

Unleashed

Persnickety

Iced tea

Hungry

The lunch experiment

Last choice

This is not what I ordered

Frogmen

Key

The message got lost somewhere

Trunk

Bridesmaid syndrome

Medieval

Mutant

4:02 A.M.

I couldn't tell if it was a costume

Sick city

Broke

Fill the sky

Spider

Island

Root

Brood

Piece

Monkey in the middle

Bad business

A borrowed sweater

Float

Crack

Moving day

Dividing line

Blow

Leftovers

The appropriate vegetable

She dug through the garbage

Field

He dreaded the approach of the bus

Rock

A bowl of cherries

Wrong turn

Blackout

One full minute

The hidden box

Drive

Bad reception

Crowded with ghosts

The long war

Wave

Exclusive

Three unlikely friends

Board

The flowers kept arriving

The next bus

Brick

The room we don't use

A change in the weather

Her shoes were the first clue

Miss

It rolled under the couch

A different ticket

Dunk

She discarded the bracelet

Leaving the party

A minor explosion

Too fast

Shelter

The water surged forward

Thirty angry mothers

Hoop
This is where it ends
Under the snow
Jungle
The window slammed shut
Never enough time
This gift has to be returned
Face
I counted five colors
The kids were having none of it
Fast
Change
Weak in the knees
He didn't recognize the language
The envelope sat on the table
Fair
Outside the frame
A prejudiced referee
Pulled from the pile
We first smelled it on a Thursday
Changed the whole dynamic of the group
The spoon fell out
I told him a thousand times
The desk drawer hadn't been opened in years
A wasted education
Stuff

Breakthroughs

Loafing is the most productive part of a writer's life.

—James Norman Hall

Incandescent

Random blood test

Track

I watched the hair fall to the floor

Glass

Step

Scene

Florida

Wake

I was the only one in the room who

Hand out

Fill

His arm brushed against

Steep

Shattered the ice

Brought me back

What is that sound?

Bar

An angel on a skateboard

I wondered about the people across the street

Why didn't I?

Unofficial landmark

Salad

The first thing I noticed about him was

The car was going 80 when we

Keep digging

Not my territory

The reason he carried a knapsack

A deserted mall

Access

What those sneakers really meant

Worm

Everyone scattered

A crumpled ticket

He didn't remember falling

I found it at a garage sale

Punch

When the bell rang

 Breakthroughs

Patience is needed with everyone,
but first of all with ourselves.

—St. Francis de Sales

When it comes right down to it, all it takes to break through from not-writing to writing is ... writing. So sit at your keyboard or pick up a pen, and start putting words on a page. What's going to happen—you'll write something bad? If it's bad, you can throw it away. But it might turn out good. It might even turn out great.

The Least You Need to Know

- Writer's block is a temporary problem—and you can beat it.
- To be a writer, all you need to do is write.
- A book of a thousand pages begins with a single word.

Good Reading for Writers

Even after you've beaten your writer's block, you can't spend every minute of the day writing. You have to read, too! In this appendix, I give you some good choices to stick your nose into when you're looking for instruction, ideas, and inspiration from other's people's writing. Just remember not to use them as an excuse to avoid your own writing desk!

Magazines for Writers

A subscription to these magazines will help ensure that you get a reminder to write at least every month or so …

Writer's Digest
This magazine offers a mix of practical advice and inspiration and covers a wide range of genres. It addresses skills like plotting and character building as well as the commercial aspects of dealing with agents and publishers. The company also puts out numerous books, including the essential *Writer's Market* annual reference and a number of spin-offs such as *Poet's Market* and *Children's Writer's and Illustrator's Market*.

Poets & Writers

Oriented more toward the "literary" arena, and with significant space dedicated to poetry, this is an extremely useful publication for those whose work doesn't fit into a particular category or is a little less mainstream. Each issue offers extensive, detailed listings of competitions, conferences, and grants, and is full of thoughtful, in-depth articles and profiles of both established and up-and-coming talents.

Showcases of Contemporary Writing

Keep up with the best stuff out there—these are just a handful of excellent, wide-ranging publications worth taking a look at if you haven't already:

The Threepenny Review
Short stories and poetry.

Tin House
Short stories and poetry.

Poetry
You guessed it, poetry (and some great essays on poetry, too). *Poetry* also publishes an annual humor issue and has the added advantage of a low cover price compared to many other journals. Hey, we starving poets have to think about these things!

The Atlantic
Nonfiction, mostly about national and world events. Sadly, *The Atlantic* no longer includes the short stories it used to be famous for, but it does put out an annual fiction issue featuring some of today's best authors.

The New York Times Magazine
Published each Sunday, this might be the best source for compelling, in-depth general-interest nonfiction out there. It makes learning about all kinds of things—from science to economics to foreign policy—not only painless, but fascinating.

The New Yorker
Fiction, nonfiction, and poetry. And, of course, cartoons.

Books About Writing

There are approximately 12 bazillion books for writers out there (12 bazillion and 1, when this one comes out). These are some of the very best I can recommend:

100 Things Every Writer Needs to Know
by Scott Edelstein
Quick-hit, highly practical, fluff-free advice from an industry insider.

The Artist's Way
by Julia Cameron
A classic creativity guide, with a spiritual, self-help vibe, that can guide you to real breakthroughs when you're suffering through a serious emotional block.

The Midnight Disease
by Alice W. Flaherty
An unusual and fun-to-read look at writer's block and other aspects of creativity from a neurologist's point of view.

Writing Down the Bones
by Natalie Goldberg
This much-loved favorite has a friendly, encouraging voice and could be alternately titled *The Zen of Writing*.

Bird by Bird
by Anne Lamott
Also a favorite of writers, this is a personal, candid, and entertaining meditation on the creative life.

On Writing
by Stephen King
The master mixes to-the-point advice for writers with his own reminiscences about his life and career.

The Forest for the Trees
by Betsy Lerner
An experienced editor focuses on both the business of publishing and the psychology of writers for an interesting and enlightening behind-the-scenes read.

The Poetry Home Repair Manual
by Ted Kooser
Accessible, truthful words of wisdom from an acclaimed—and utterly unpretentious—poet.

A Poetry Handbook
by Mary Oliver
Know your anapest from your elbow with this introduction to the basics that offers clear information on everything from line breaks to meter to imagery.

Best Words, Best Order
by Stephen Dobyns
A more challenging read than the preceding titles,
this is an excellent volume of essays for anyone
wanting an in-depth understanding of poetry.

And a Few Enthusiastic Recommendations

Because nothing inspires and instructs like great
writing does!

The Shell Collector by Anthony Doerr

Never Let Me Go by Kazuo Ishiguro

Motherless Brooklyn by Jonathan Lethem

Back When We Were Grownups by Anne Tyler

Digging to America by Anne Tyler

Charming Billy by Alice McDermott

Pallbearers Envying the One Who Rides by
Stephen Dobyns

The Cradle Place by Thomas Lux

Bee Season by Myla Goldberg

Wickett's Remedy by Myla Goldberg

The Night of Falling Stars by J. Robert Lennon

The Funnies by J. Robert Lennon

The Fourth Hand by John Irving

Drinking Coffee Elsewhere by ZZ Packer

Nickel and Dimed by Barbara Ehrenreich

Bait and Switch by Barbara Ehrenreich

The Perfect Storm by Sebastian Junger

Generation Kill by Evan Wright

The Russian Debutante's Notebook by Gary Shteyngart

Absurdistan by Gary Shteyngart

Wolves Eat Dogs by Martin Cruz Smith

Gorky Park by Martin Cruz Smith

Ariel by Sylvia Plath

New and Selected Poems by Michael Ryan

Ants on the Melon by Virginia Hamilton Adair

Expecting Adam by Martha Beck

Hypocrite in a Pouffy White Dress by Susan Jane Gilman

Secondhand Smoke by Patty Friedmann

1984 by George Orwell

The Wishbones by Tom Perrotta

The Partly Cloudy Patriot by Sarah Vowell

Index

D

R